101 Things To Do Before You Die

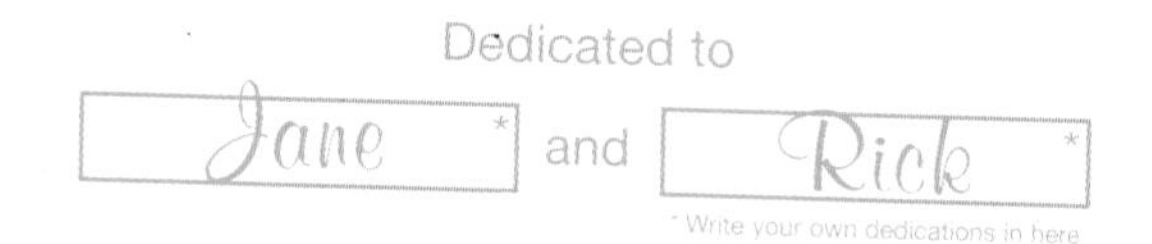

First published in Great Britain in 2004

Bloomsbury Publishing, Plc, 38 Soho Square, London W1D 3HB

A CIP catalogue record for this book is available from the British Library

ISBN 07475 7390 5

1 3 5 7 9 10 8 6 4 2

Printed in China by C&C Offset Printing Co., Ltd.

All papers used by Bloomsbury Publishing are natural, recyclable products made from wood grown in well-managed forests. The manufacturing processes conform to the environmental regulations of the country of origin.

101 Things To Do Before You Die

Write your name here

Written, designed and illustrated by Richard Horne

B L O O M S B U R Y

Introduction

Lists. We all have them. Instead of grocery lists, why not chart all the things we'd like to achieve in our lives? Here is a way to chart your sporting triumphs, your sexual misadventures, your lifetime struggles and your reckless behaviour. What follows is a list of **101 Things To Do Before You Die**. Some you might have already done, some you've always wanted to do and some you'll have to wait a lifetime to do. Use this book as a supplement to your own **Things To Do** list.

Attempt

Travel the world in search of the ultimate adventure sports, bungee jump, sky dive and scuba dive. Catch a fish with your bare hands while skinny dipping at midnight, cook it to your own perfected recipe on a fire you made without matches.

Complete

Track your lifetime achievements by filling in these easy-to-follow forms.

Expire

It's better to regret something you have done, rather than to regret something you should have done but didn't. Living is the middle bit between life and death, it's what you do in the middle that counts. Start now ...

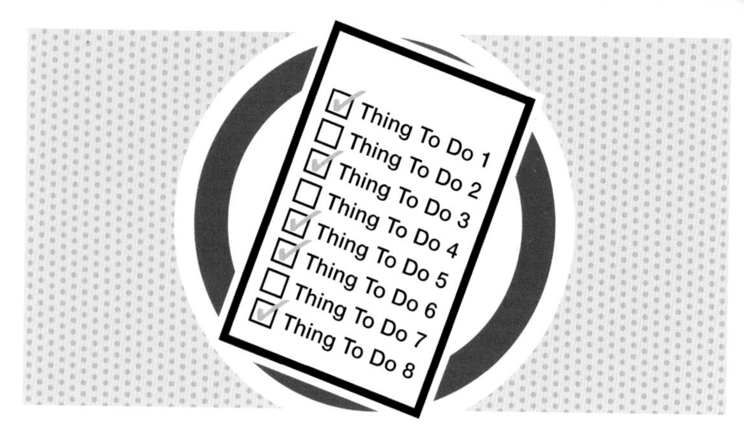

How To Use This Book

The concept is simple. Accomplish the **101 Things To Do Before You Die**, tick the boxes and fill in the form as you go.

Form Usage

- Enter your information frankly and truthfully - if you don't tell the truth you'll only be lying to yourself
- You may find some of the forms too small for all the information you'd like to enter. To solve this you can copy the extra pages at the back of the book or visit the website for extra pages, duplicate pages and larger maps at **www.101thingstodo.co.uk**

Your **Things To Do**

- If there are **Things To Do** you'd like to do that aren't mentioned in the book, add your top ten **Things To Do** on the pages provided at the back

Helpful Tips

- Use the following rules as a guideline to completing the **Things To Do**

101 Things To Do Before You Die

Rules

 Perform as many **Things To Do** as possible in your lifetime.

 Always carry this book with you (a **Thing To Do** may present itself at an unexpected moment).

 Take risks. Some of the **Things To Do** in this book cannot be accomplished without a little courage.

 Be creative. It may take a bit of ingenuity to complete some of the **Things To Do**.

 Be patient. Some **Things To Do** can't be completed until later in life.

 Be quick. Fill out the form as soon as you've completed a **Thing To Do,** before you forget the details.

 If at first you don't succeed, keep trying. Some **Things To Do** may take a few attempts to complete.

 Push yourself. Do things you would normally avoid doing.

 Above all, have fun. The **Things To Do** are a supplement to your daily life.

 Take the opportunity.

Some Things You Will Need

Here is a list of some of the items you will need to complete the **101 Things To Do Before You Die**. You don't need to have them all before you start, but it would be advisable to at least have a pen, a pair of scissors, glue, a camera, access to a photocopier and money handy. You can acquire the other items as you continue through the list – some items will be provided for you – but forward planning, spontaneity, a head for heights, a reckless spirit, a sense of humour, a good imagination and optimism is down to you.

☐ A Pen
☐ A Pair of Scissors
☐ Glue
☐ Money
☐ A Camera
☐ A Photocopier
☐ A Pack of Cards
☐ Poker Chips
☐ A Strong Stomach
☐ Some Strangers
☐ Some Friends
☐ A Partner
☐ Beer
☐ A Head for Heights
☐ Skills
☐ A Reckless Spirit
☐ Betting Slips
☐ A Driving Licence
☐ A World Map
☐ A Local Map
☐ Condoms
☐ Clothes
☐ No Clothes
☐ Alcohol
☐ A Dart
☐ An Instrument
☐ A Stick of Chalk
☐ A Balaclava or Ski Mask
☐ A Celebrity
☐ A Rock Star
☐ A Confessional Booth
☐ An Understanding Vicar
☐ Spray Cans
☐ A Van
☐ A Fast Car
☐ Various Animals
☐ A Bucket
☐ Christmas Decorations
☐ An Amusement Park
☐ A Space Shuttle
☐ Junk
☐ Talent
☐ The *Kama Sutra*
☐ A Passport
☐ Luck
☐ Patience
☐ A Need for Speed
☐ A Video or DVD Player
☐ A Television
☐ A Trip to the Cinema
☐ Clear Skies
☐ The Sun
☐ The Moon
☐ The Stars
☐ A Video Camera
☐ Fruit
☐ Batteries
☐ A Good Imagination
☐ A Golf Club
☐ A Golf Ball
☐ A Suit / Outfit
☐ A Football
☐ Forward Planning
☐ Spontaneity
☐ A Sense of Humour
☐ Optimism

101 Things To Do Before You Die

Important Information

WARNING: WHEN EMBARKING ON THE 101 THINGS TO DO BEFORE YOU DIE YOU DO SO AT YOUR OWN RISK.

PROCEED ONLY UNDER COMPETENT SUPERVISION.

THE AUTHOR AND PUBLISHER ACCEPT NO RESPONSIBILITY FOR ANY ACCIDENTS OR INJURIES WHICH MAY OCCUR DURING ATTEMPTS TO COMPLETE ANY OF THE 101 THINGS TO DO BEFORE YOU DIE.

IF YOU AGREE WITH THESE TERMS PLEASE SIGN BELOW.

Sign here

101 Things To Do Before You Die

The List

1 ☐ Write a Best-seller
2 ☐ Swim With ...
3 ☐ Win an Award, Trophy or Prize
4 ☐ Catch a Fish With Your Bare Hands
5 ☐ Make a Discovery
6 ☐ Throw a House Party When Your Parents Are Out
7 ☐ Be Part of a Threesome
8 ☐ Realise Your Childhood Dream
9 ☐ Learn That Instrument
10 ☐ Leave Your Mark in Graffiti
11 ☐ Storm Chase a Tornado
12 ☐ Get a Piece of Art into an Exhibition
13 ☐ Meet Someone with Your Own Name
14 ☐ Ride the World's Biggest Rollercoasters
15 ☐ Stage Dive or Crowd Surf
16 ☐ Get into the *Guinness Book of World Records*
17 ☐ Own a Pointless Collection
18 ☐ Study the *Kama Sutra* and Put Theory into Practice
19 ☐ Master Poker and Win Big in a Casino
20 ☐ Get Backstage and Get Off with a Rock God
21 ☐ Be a Human Guinea Pig
22 ☐ Go Up in a Hot Air Balloon
23 ☐ Get Arrested
24 ☐ See a Space Shuttle Launch
25 ☐ Capture the Moment in an Award-winning Photograph
26 ☐ Bungee Jump
27 ☐ See an Erupting Volcano
28 ☐ Sky Dive
29 ☐ Meet Your Idol
30 ☐ Stay in the Best Suite in a Five Star Hotel
31 ☐ Experience Weightlessness
32 ☐ See the Aurora Borealis
33 ☐ Get to Score a Hole in One
34 ☐ Design Your Own Cocktail
35 ☐ Play a Part in Your Favourite TV Show
36 ☐ Visit Every Country
37 ☐ Make Fire Without Matches
38 ☐ See These Animals in the Wild...
39 ☐ Go to the Dogs
40 ☐ Get a Free Upgrade on a Plane
41 ☐ Be Friends With Your Ex
42 ☐ Hit Your Targets
43 ☐ Throw a Dart into a Map and Travel to Where it Lands
44 ☐ Attend a Film Premiere
45 ☐ Do a Runner From a Fancy Restaurant
46 ☐ Scuba Dive
47 ☐ Milk a Cow
48 ☐ Be Present When Your Country Wins the World Cup
49 ☐ See Both Solar and Lunar Eclipses
50 ☐ Write Your Name Over a Star on the Walk of Fame
51 ☐ Learn Another Language
52 ☐ Read the Greatest Books Ever Written

101 Things To Do Before You Die

The List

53 ☐ Complete a Coast to Coast Road Trip Across America
54 ☐ Make at Least One Huge Purchase You Can't Afford
55 ☐ Score the Winning Goal / Try / Basket
56 ☐ Gatecrash a Fancy Party
57 ☐ See the All-time Greatest Films
58 ☐ Live in the Place You Love
59 ☐ Leave a Job You Hate
60 ☐ Take Part in an Police Line-up
61 ☐ Get Away with the Perfect Practical Joke or Hoax
62 ☐ Join the Mile High Club
63 ☐ Make the Front Page of a National Newspaper
64 ☐ Drive a Car at Top Speed
65 ☐ Shout 'Drinks Are on Me!' in a Pub or a Bar
66 ☐ Be Part of a Flash Mob
67 ☐ Visit ...
68 ☐ Save Someone's Life
69 ☐ In Various Languages, Learn to ...
70 ☐ Invent a Word That Makes it into the Dictionary
71 ☐ Have Adventurous Sex
72 ☐ Have Enough Money to Do All the Things on This List
73 ☐ Stand on the International Date Line
74 ☐ Learn to Fly a Plane
75 ☐ Get a Tattoo and/or a Piercing
76 ☐ Invent Something
77 ☐ Learn Astronomy and Read the Night Sky
78 ☐ Drink a Vintage Wine
79 ☐ Answer a Personal Ad
80 ☐ Spend Christmas on the Beach
81 ☐ Get Barred From a Pub or Bar
82 ☐ Build Your Own House
83 ☐ Skinny Dip at Midnight
84 ☐ Sell All Your Junk on eBay and Make a Profit
85 ☐ Visit the World's Tallest Buildings
86 ☐ Run a Marathon
87 ☐ Conquer Your Fear
88 ☐ Get Married Unusually
89 ☐ Throw Away the Instant Noodles
90 ☐ Join the 16-Mile High Club
91 ☐ Publish a Cult Website
92 ☐ Own an Original Work of Art
93 ☐ Complete the Monopoly Board Pub Crawl
94 ☐ Get Something Named After You
95 ☐ Get Revenge
96 ☐ Be an Extra in a Film
97 ☐ Live Out of a Van
98 ☐ Go on a Demonstration
99 ☐ Confess
100 ☐ Reach 100 Years of Age
101 ☐ Continue Your Gene Pool

Start Your Novel Here

Write a Best-seller

This is the perfect **Thing To Do** to start with. This is your book. Your name is on the front, these are all your achievements and accomplishments. This book is a catalogue of your life story in a series of events; you could fill in the achieved star for this **Thing To Do** right now (although you won't reap the financial benefits that come with it). The best thing you can do is write your own book from all those ideas you've got tucked away inside you somewhere.

Your Light Bulb Moment

It can happen anywhere and at any time; once it does you can't shake it. You might already have your idea, but you just haven't had the time to develop it. Write in your spare time, in your lunch break at work or give up your job and play at being a full-time author. Keep a pad and a pen by your bed at all times.

Where and When Was Your Light Bulb Moment?

Once Published
Ask your family and friends to buy your book; this way you can push yourself up the best-seller list. Leave your book open to a sequel (even the Bible had a sequel).

Write a Best-seller **Form**

Once you have completed this **Thing To Do**, stick your Achieved Star here and fill in the form

Achieved

What is the title of your book?

How long did it take to write?

Years Months Days

In which category does your book appear?

Fiction | Non Fiction | Biog | Autobiog | Children's | Humour | Ref | Other

What is your book about? Write a brief synopsis

Has your book been published yet?

y/n If yes, when? d d m m y y y y

What is the name of your publisher?

How long had you been trying for a book deal?

Years Months Days

Did you receive an advance? How much was it?

FATCAT PUBLISHING CHEQUE

to:

£/$

Did you get royalties?

y/n If yes, what is your percentage? %

What was the size of the first print run?

Has the book been reprinted? y/n

What is the Recommended Retail Price of your book? THINGS TO DO £/$

Was there a launch party? If yes, where was it?

y/n

What were the reviews for your book like?

Poor | OK | Good | Very Good | Excellent

Did it make the Best-seller list? Position and date

If yes, when? d d m m y y y y

How many copies in total has your book sold?

0 - 999 | 1,000 9,999 | 10,000 49,999 | 50,000 99,999 | 100,000 149,999 | 150,000 499,999 | 500,000 999,999 | A million and over

How many countries has it been published in?

Have you left your book open to a sequel? y/n

At the same time you could complete this **Thing To Do**

03: Win an Award, Trophy or Prize • 63: Make the Front Page of a National Newspaper • 72: Have Enough Money to Do All the Things on This List

Swim With ...

The scariest, the biggest, the most intelligent and the most colourful creatures in the sea.

Sharks

If you find yourself swimming with sharks, make sure it's out of choice rather than by accident. If it is by accident, make sure you are swimming away from the end with teeth.

Whales

Remember, size isn't important.

Dolphins

If a ball falls out of your boat and needs returning or there is a hoop that you need jumped through, if you find a dolphin, they'll help you out. But don't be fooled – they're not all like Flipper.

Tropical Fish

Be wary of piranha.

Good Places to See ... Great White Sharks – **South Africa** and **Adelaide** • Hammerhead Sharks – **Galapagos Islands** • Humpback Whales – **Tonga** • Killer Whales – **Canada** • Bottle Nosed Dolphins – **Hawaii, Florida** and **Scotland** • Tropical Fish – **Great Barrier Reef**

Swim With Sharks, Whales, Dolphins and Tropical Fish **Form**

Once you have completed this **Thing To Do**, stick your Achieved Star here and fill in the form

Achieved

Shark. What kind of shark was it?

Date and time

d d m m y y y y :

Where were you?

Did you see more than one? y/n If yes, how many? Would you swim with them again? y/n

How close did you get? Circle the correct answer

I got to touch it | touching distance | 2 metres | 5 metres | far too close | close enough | nowhere near it | saw it from a boat

Whale. What kind of whale was it?

Date and time

d d m m y y y y :

Where were you?

Did you see more than one? y/n If yes, how many? Would you swim with them again? y/n

How close did you get? Circle the correct answer

I got to touch it | touching distance | 2 metres | 5 metres | far too close | close enough | nowhere near it | saw it from a boat

Dolphin. What kind of dolphin was it?

Date and time

d d m m y y y y :

Where were you?

Did you see more than one? y/n If yes, how many? Would you swim with them again? y/n

How close did you get? Circle the correct answer

I got to touch it | touching distance | 2 metres | 5 metres | far too close | close enough | nowhere near it | saw it from a boat

Tropical Fish. What kind of fish were they?

Date and time

d d m m y y y y :

Where were you?

Did you see more than one? y/n If yes, how many? Would you swim with them again? y/n

How close did you get? Circle the correct answer

I got to touch them | touching distance | 2 metres | 5 metres | far too close | close enough | nowhere near them | saw them from a boat

At the same time you could complete these **Things To Do**
04: Catch a Fish With Your Bare Hands • 46: Scuba Dive • 71: Have Adventurous Sex • 83: Skinny Dip at Midnight

Win an Award, Trophy or Prize

Silverware on the sideboard is a way of boasting about your achievements without having to say 'I did that!' out loud. It is also a way to show your children that there used to be more to you than shouting and pocket money.

If you've never won an award, wait until you retire, then take up an OAP's activity such as ballroom dancing. As long as you are younger and fitter than the other pensioners, you'll clean up. If all else fails, get a bogus award made: 'Champion Emu Rider' or 'World's Tallest Person'. Nobody will argue, you've got the trophy to prove it.

The Winner Takes it All

If you have won more than one award, fill in the certificate for the Award you're most proud of and list the other awards you've achieved in the 'Other Awards I've Won' column provided.

Whatever you do, make sure one of the awards you win isn't the **Darwin Award**.

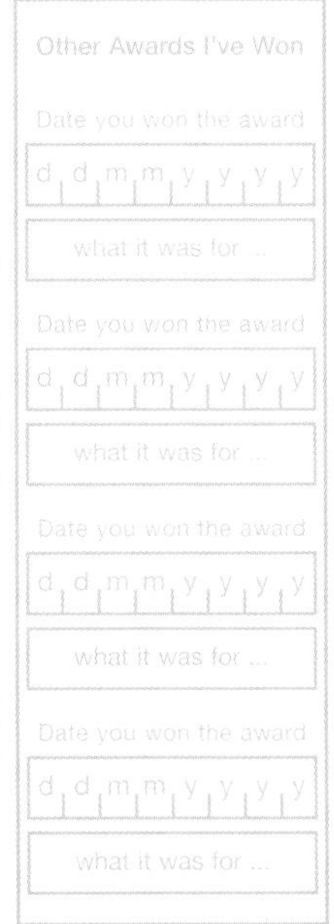

The Darwin Award
This award is given posthumously every year to the people who died in the most ridiculous way through their own carelessness. Natural human selection through stupidity.

Win an Award, Trophy or Prize **Form**

Once you have completed this **Thing To Do**, stick your Achieved Star here and fill in the form

Achieved

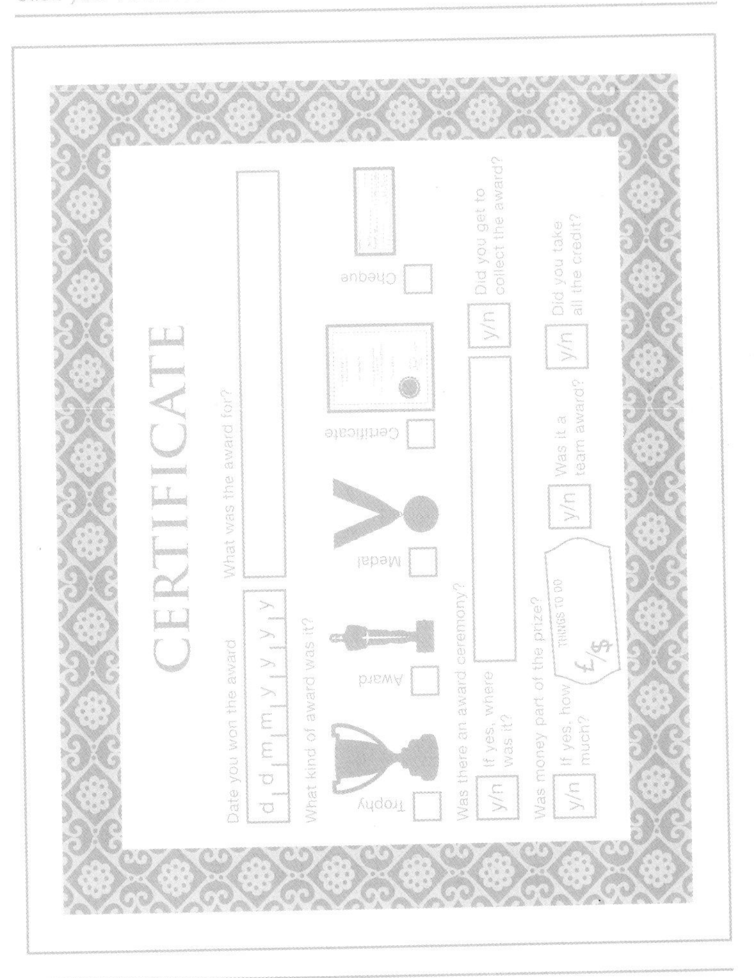

CERTIFICATE
Date you won the award
d d m m y y y y
What was the award for?
What kind of award was it?
Trophy
Award
Medal
Certificate
Cheque
Was there an award ceremony?
y/n
If yes, where was it?
y/n
Did you get to collect the award?
Was money part of the prize?
y/n
If yes, how much?
£/$
y/n
Was it a team award?
y/n
Did you take all the credit?

At the same time you could complete these **Things To Do**
16: Get into the *Guinness Book of World Records* • 55: Score the Winning Goal/Try/Basket • 63: Make the Front Page of a National Newspaper

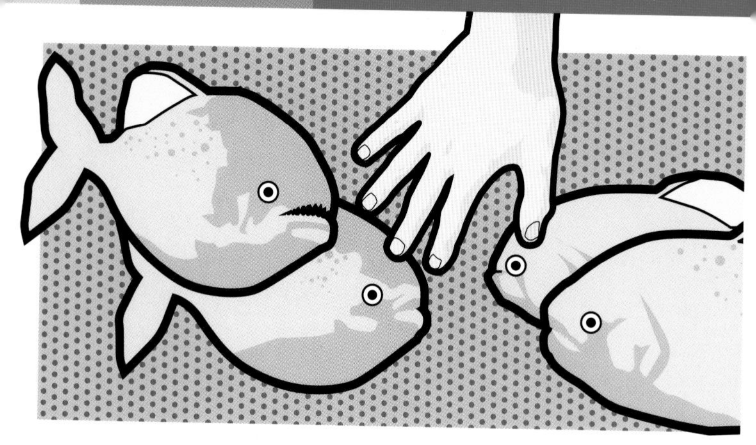

Catch a Fish With Your Bare Hands

Anyone can catch a fish with a fishing rod or a net, it's far too easy. If you're fishing with a rod, all you need to do is set up your equipment, take a nap, and wait until the fish gives itself up for you. Where's the fun in that? On the other hand, catching a fish with your bare hands takes skill, patience, it gives the fish more of a sporting chance and you more of a challenge. What you need to do is get practising.

Catch Me If You Can

- Get your hands used to cold. You'll need to be able to withstand the icy temperatures of the water
- Choose clear shallow water. Good knowledge of the best streams for fish is essential otherwise you're wasting your time
- When you see your target, slowly get into a position behind the fish without splashing or any sudden movements
- Move your hands slowly around the fish; once your hands are in position, snatch the fish, and hang on tight
- If the fish gets away, keep trying; if you catch him, eat him with a nice slice of lemon. It tastes all the sweeter in the knowledge that you caught it in your own bare hands

Other Creatures to Catch
A cow with a lasso, a butterfly with a net, an escaped hamster, a cat that needs to be taken to the vet's and a fly with chopsticks.

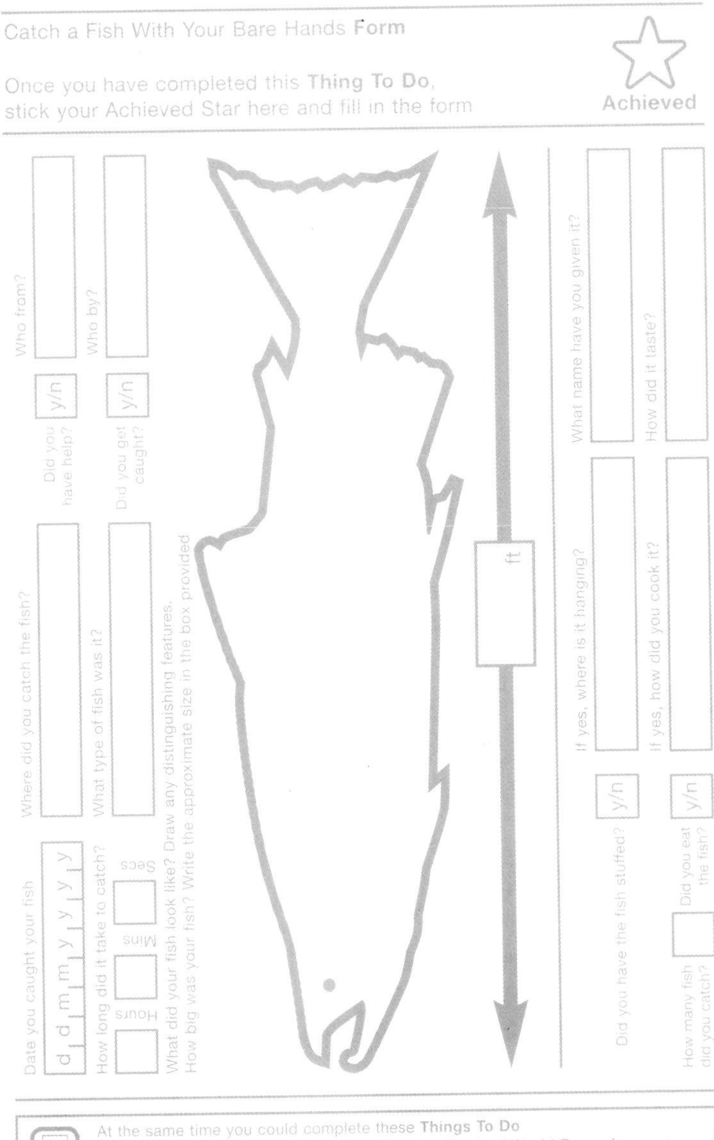

Catch a Fish With Your Bare Hands **Form**

Once you have completed this **Thing To Do**, stick your Achieved Star here and fill in the form

Achieved

Date you caught your fish d d m m y y y y

How long did it take to catch? Hours Mins Secs

Where did you catch the fish?

What type of fish was it?

Did you have help? y/n

Who from?

Did you get caught? y/n

Who by?

What did your fish look like? Draw any distinguishing features. How big was your fish? Write the approximate size in the box provided

ft

What name have you given it?

Did you have the fish stuffed? y/n

If yes, where is it hanging?

Did you eat the fish? y/n

If yes, how did you cook it?

How did it taste?

How many fish did you catch?

At the same time you could complete these **Things To Do**
02: Swim With ... • 16: Get into the *Guinness Book of World Records* •
23: Get Arrested • 83: Skinny Dip at Midnight

Make a Discovery

Not only is it possible to discover new species; it's also possible to discover old ones. In 1938, off the eastern coast of South Africa, a living fossil was discovered. The Coelacanth, an ancient prehistoric fish which was thought to have become extinct over 65 million years ago, was discovered alive and unchanged over millions of years of evolution. Since its initial discovery, more and more Coelacanth have been discovered and colonies of them have been found near the Comoros islands off the coast of Africa and off the island of Sulawesi, Indonesia.

Whatever your discovery may be, make sure it is named after you (see **Thing To Do** No. 94).

I Still Haven't Found What I'm Looking For

- New Species – The rain forests and the deep oceans are the best places to find the majority of the world's undiscovered species
- Space – Look to the skies for proof of new planets (see Sedna), new stars, worm holes, parallel universes, UFOs and aliens
- A New Theory – Discover a new theory and spend the rest of your life trying to prove it really does work

Still to be Discovered or Proven The Meaning of Life • What happened before the Big Bang • Whether time travel is possible • If String Theory is correct • Extra-terrestrials • The Loch Ness Monster • The Yeti

Make a Discovery **Form**

Once you have completed this **Thing To Do**, stick your Achieved Star here and fill in the form

Achieved

Date and time

d d m m y y y y :

y/n Did you get the credit and recognition you deserved for your discovery?

Describe your discovery

If no, what happened? Who took your credit?

Which category does your discovery fall into?

Theory, New Species, Archaeological, Medical, Talent, Other

How did you come across your discovery?

Years of Study, Hard work, Accident, Found it, Stole it, Other

Where did the discovery occur?

What is the name of your discovery?

How long did it take to discover?

Years Months Days

Have you earned money from your discovery? If so, how much?

THINGS TO DO £/$

Draw your discovery in area provided below

At the same time you could complete these **Things To Do**
03: Win an Award, Trophy or Prize • 08: Realise Your Childhood Dream • 21: Be a Human Guinea Pig • 94: Get Something Named After You

Throw a House Party When Your Parents Are Out

Birthdays, Christmas, Moving house, Births, Deaths. Any excuse is a great excuse for a party, as long as you've managed to remove the Big Brother threat of your parents first.

You want a party with drink/drugs/loud music/dancing/sex*. Your parents want a party with crisps, jelly and an early finish at 9.30pm. You're not going to get what you want with your parents around. Face it, they've gotta go.

There is only one answer: dishonesty. What the eye doesn't see, the heart doesn't grieve. You've got to go behind their backs. It's the only way.

It might take weeks, months or even years to find the right opportunity to host your party while they're away, but it'll be worth it. Make up a bogus function for them to attend, arrange for them to stay with relatives, even send them on holiday, just get rid of them.

As long as you realise that if anything is broken or missing it's down to you to explain. But nothing is going to go wrong, right?

* delete where applicable

Party Tips Make sure your parents have filled up the drinks cabinet before they go away. Fill up half empty liquor bottles with water for Vodka and Gin, cold tea for Whisky. Blame untidiness and breakages on burglars.

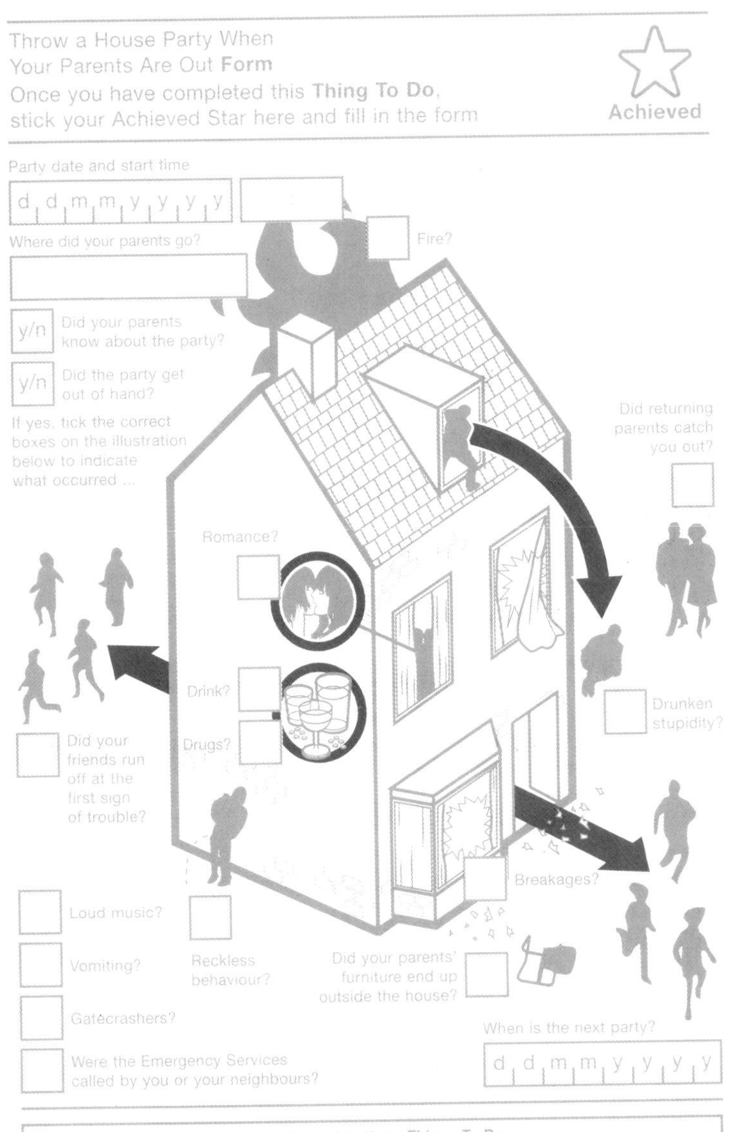

Throw a House Party When Your Parents Are Out **Form**

Once you have completed this **Thing To Do**, stick your Achieved Star here and fill in the form

Achieved

Party date and start time

d d m m y y y y

Where did your parents go?

y/n Did your parents know about the party?

y/n Did the party get out of hand?

If yes, tick the correct boxes on the illustration below to indicate what occurred ...

Fire?

Did returning parents catch you out?

Romance?

Drink?

Drugs?

Drunken stupidity?

Did your friends run off at the first sign of trouble?

Breakages?

Loud music?

Vomiting?

Reckless behaviour?

Did your parents' furniture end up outside the house?

Gatecrashers?

Were the Emergency Services called by you or your neighbours?

When is the next party?

d d m m y y y y

At the same time you could complete these **Things To Do**

07: Be Part of a Threesome • 23: Get Arrested • 34: Design Your Own Cocktail • 78: Drink a Vintage Wine

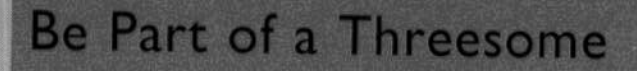

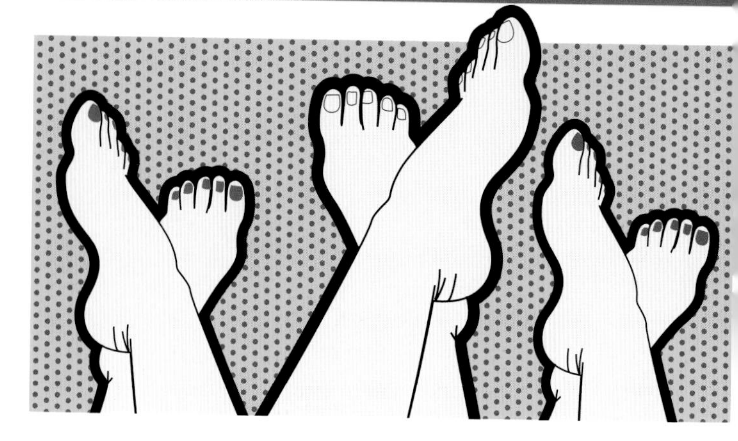

Be Part of a Threesome

Three's a crowd? Not in this case.

Threesome
A sexual experience involving three people. A sexual fantasy favourite usually made reality when fuelled by alcohol.

Stuck in the Middle With You

- Drink alcohol; alcohol banishes inhibitions and contributes to threesome fun. As long as all parties are willing, turn an average evening into a great one
- Turn ordinary games into ones where clothes come off. Strip poker, strip Twister, strip darts. Basically think of any game and put the word 'strip' in front of it
- If someone comes back to the house unexpectedly, try to get dressed in record time. Try to put on all the correct clothes
- Warning! Flailing limbs can cause serious harm

Threesome, A Golf Term

In golf, a threesome is a match in which two players play alternate strokes with the same ball, while they take on another player, two against one

It also means three players within the same round

Turn your golf threesome into the other definition of the word, this way you could accomplish two **Things To Do** at once (see **Thing To Do** No. 33)

Be discreet or else you could complete a third **Thing To Do**, get arrested (see **Thing To Do** No. 23)

Three, is the Magic Number
Degrees • Musketeers • Amigos • Wise Men • Stooges • Blind Mice • Billy Goats Gruff • Legged Race • of a Kind • D • French Hens • Men and a Baby • Coins in a Fountain

Be Part of a Threesome **Form**

Once you have completed this **Thing To Do**, stick your Achieved Star here and fill in the form

Achieved

Date and time

d d m m y y y y | :

Where were you?

Which combination were you involved in?

Girl Boy Girl — Boy Girl Boy — Girl Girl Girl — Boy Boy Boy

Name the other two people involved

m/f | write person 2's name here

m/f | write person 3's name here

How did the situation occur?

Was alcohol involved? y/n

Were drugs involved? y/n

Where the other two involved friends?

y/n If no, how long had you known them before threeway action occurred?

I have known person 2 for [ ] Minutes / Hours / Days

I have known person 3 for [ ] Minutes / Hours / Days

Where there more than 3 people involved?

If yes, how many other people were involved?

Who were the other people?

m/f | write person 4's name here

m/f | write person 5's name here

m/f | write person 6's name here

Was it fun? y/n If no ...

Have there been complications since? y/n If yes, what's happened?

Has it happened again since?

y/n If no, would you like it to? y/n

At the same time you could complete these **Things To Do**
18: Study the *Kama Sutra* and Put Theory into Practice • 20: Get Backstage and Get Off with a Rock God • 71: Have Adventurous Sex • 101: Continue Your Gene Pool

Realise Your Childhood Dream

No matter how unrealistic some childhood dreams seem to be, they can still be possible. On 6 May 2001, Dennis Tito became the world's first space tourist. To do so he had to fly to Russia, commit to six months' training and pay £14 million of his own money to cover the costs, but he managed it – he fulfilled his childhood dream and became an astronaut.

Space travel is a childhood dream for thousands of people but unless you're a multi-millionaire like Dennis with six months and £14 million to spare, keep on dreaming. But if it wasn't for the Wright Brothers' childhood dream to fly, then Dennis Tito wouldn't have even had the opportunity, he'd still be dreaming like the rest of us.

There are plenty of other childhood dreams that aren't as outlandish as travelling into space, that cost a lot less and don't take as much time. So you've still got time to work for Lego, be a stormtrooper, score a goal in the World Cup and have your own pony.

Dream On One third of our life is spent sleeping; this amounts to six years of dreaming. Every night we dream for an average of two to three hours. Even if you don't think you dream, you do.

Realise Your Childhood Dream **Form**

Once you have completed this **Thing To Do**,
stick your Achieved Star here and fill in the form

Achieved

Draw and describe your childhood dream in the thought bubble below

Date you completed your dream

d d m m y y y y

Was it as fun as you expected?

How old were you when you completed your dream? yrs

Is your childhood dream now your permanent job? y/n

Describe the day you realise your childhood dream and attach a photo

At the same time you could complete these **Things To Do**
29: Meet Your Idol • 31: Experience Weightlessness • 48: Be Present When Your Country Wins the World Cup • 55: Score the Winning Goal / Try / Basket

Learn That Instrument

People fall into two categories: those that had after-school music lessons and those that didn't. With hindsight, those that didn't wish they had, and those that did wished they hadn't at the time but now are glad they did.

While your friends were playing outside, you were inside. You told your parents you didn't want to go but they keep making you. You faked illness, said you 'forgot' or just didn't come home. The lessons drag on and on and after numerous protests your parents finally give in. They said 'You'll thank us for it one day'; at the time you didn't believe them, but now you know that they were right all along, and since you've benefited musically you can be sure you're going to inflict the same pain upon your children. Make them perform for the whole family every Christmas; they'll thank you for it one day, especially when they discover the volume controls.

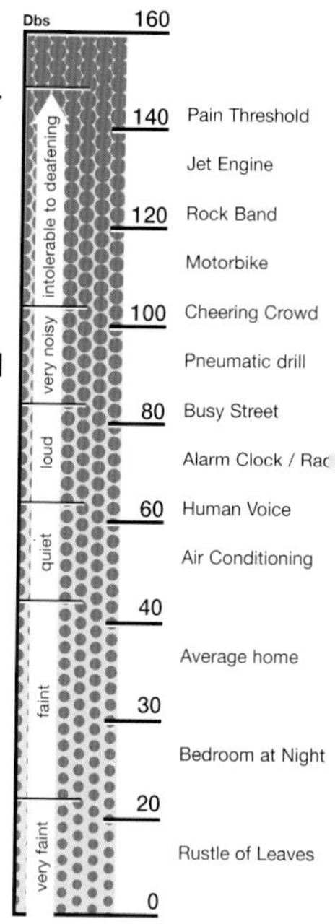

The World's Most Popular Instrument
The piano is the world's most popular instrument. It was invented in the early 1700s by Bartolomeo Cristofori in Padua, Italy, from a modified harpsichord.

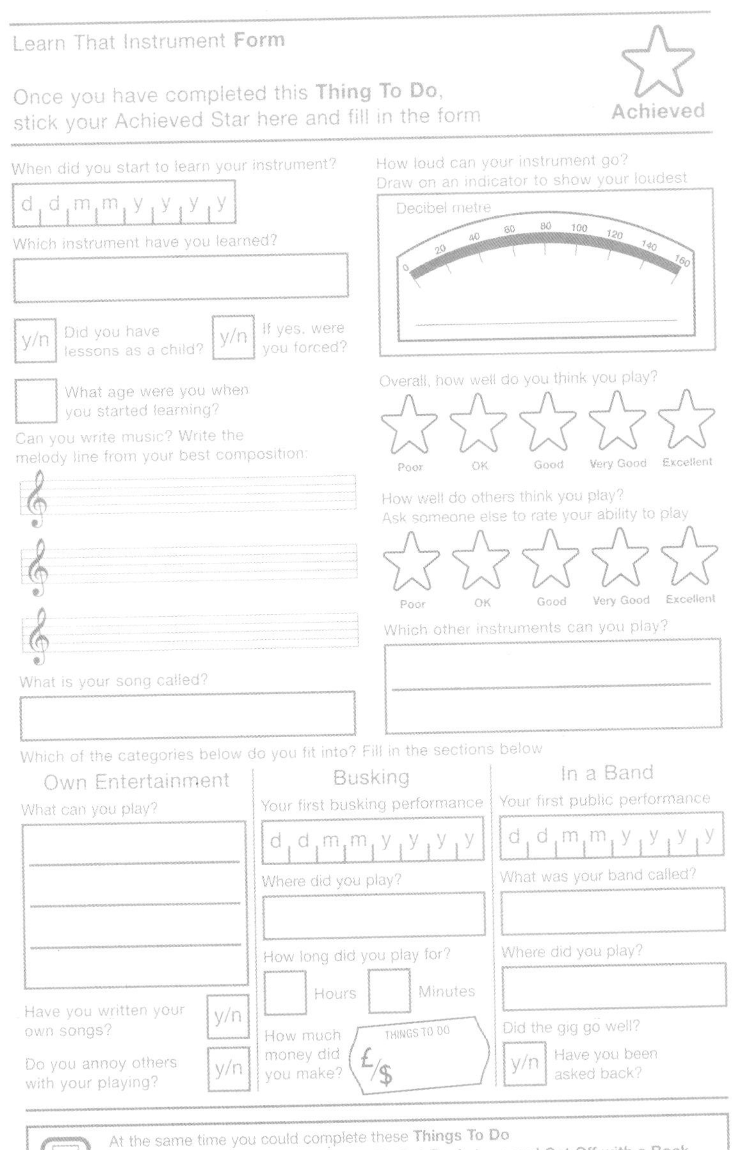

Learn That Instrument **Form**

Once you have completed this **Thing To Do**, stick your Achieved Star here and fill in the form

Achieved

When did you start to learn your instrument?

d d m m y y y y

Which instrument have you learned?

y/n Did you have lessons as a child?

y/n If yes, were you forced?

What age were you when you started learning?

Can you write music? Write the melody line from your best composition:

What is your song called?

How loud can your instrument go? Draw on an indicator to show your loudest

Overall, how well do you think you play?

Poor OK Good Very Good Excellent

How well do others think you play? Ask someone else to rate your ability to play

Poor OK Good Very Good Excellent

Which other instruments can you play?

Which of the categories below do you fit into? Fill in the sections below

Own Entertainment

What can you play?

Have you written your own songs? y/n

Do you annoy others with your playing? y/n

Busking

Your first busking performance

d d m m y y y y

Where did you play?

How long did you play for?

Hours Minutes

How much money did you make? THINGS TO DO £/$

In a Band

Your first public performance

d d m m y y y y

What was your band called?

Where did you play?

Did the gig go well?

y/n Have you been asked back?

At the same time you could complete these **Things To Do**

03: Win an Award, Trophy or Prize • 20: Get Backstage and Get Off with a Rock God • 30: Stay in the Best Suite in a Five Star Hotel • 97: Live Out of a Van

Leave Your Mark in Graffiti

Have you got something to say and no one's listening? Then spray it.

Graffiti isn't a modern practice. The Romans left their mark in public places and so did the Egyptians. Painted messages were discovered on the walls of Pompeii during its excavation. Messages such as *Lucius pinxit* (Lucius painted this) and *Suspirium puellarum Celadus thraex* (Celadus makes the girls moan) were found daubed on the walls (these are some of the printable ones) and long before the Romans, the Egyptians also left their mark, although they were made in stone with a chisel. The difference is, in those days they didn't have to creep around in the dead of night carrying their tools in a bag while wearing a balaclava or ski mask. Graffiti has been around for thousands of years and no matter what is done to combat it, it isn't going to go away. The graffiti police are hunting your thoughts down with their white paint but the blank walls are crying out for you to spread your message.

Essential Equipment

- Spray paints, pre-prepared stencils, gloves, a hooded top, a balaclava or a ski mask, a lookout, a fast pair of legs

Graffiti
The term graffiti comes from the Greek word *graphein* which means 'to write'. Graffiti was first found on ancient Roman architecture, which gave birth to the word.

Leave Your Mark in Graffiti **Form**

Once you have completed this **Thing To Do**,
stick your Achieved Star here and fill in the form

Achieved

Date and time of your graffiti

d d m m y y y y   :

Where did you leave your mark?

Recreate your message, tag and other graffiti you've been responsible for below

Did you get caught? y/n

If yes, what was your punishment?

Have you graffitied since? y/n

At the same time you could complete these **Things To Do**
03: Win an Award, Trophy or Prize • 23: Get Arrested • 36: Visit Every Country •
50: Write Your Name Over a Star on the Walk of Fame • 91: Publish a Cult Website

Storm Chase a Tornado

Cars overturned, hailstones as big as your fist, houses ripped apart and flying cows. Welcome to the world of storm-chasing.

Blowin' in the Wind

- What you need: Car, Camcorder, Camera, Maps, Mobile Phone and a Passenger
- Make sure your car is in top condition; you don't want to break down with a 250mph tornado chasing you
- If possible use a 4x4 vehicle; you never know where the unpredictable tornado is going to go next, you might have to get out of its way
- A tornado's average lifespan is about 15 minutes; you've got to be quick
- Your passenger should constantly film once you've spotted the tornado while you keep driving; try to sell the video to a national TV station
- If you do break down pray the tornado goes the other way

Fujita Scale or F-Scale

F0
Gale Tornado
Weak
40–72mph

F1
Moderate Tornado
Weak
73–112mph

F2
Significant Tornado
Strong
113–157mph

F3
Severe Tornado
Strong
158–206mph

F4
Devastating Tornado
Violent
207–260mph

F5
Incredible Tornado
Violent
261–318mph

Tornado Alley Can be found in central America, crossing the states of Alabama, Arkansas, Florida, Iowa, Kansas, Mississippi, Missouri, Nebraska, Oklahoma and Texas. There are just under 800 reported tornados a year.

Storm Chase a Tornado **Form**

Once you have completed this **Thing To Do**, stick your Achieved Star here and fill in the form

Achieved

Date d d m m y y y y

Time you saw the tornado :

Time the tornado disappeared :

Did you see flying animals? y/n

Did you or your car get hit by huge hailstones? y/n

Did you see houses destroyed? y/n

Did you see flying people? y/n

Did you see trees ripped up? y/n

Destruction of power supplies? y/n

... and explosions? y/n

What was the force of the tornado on the F-Scale?

How many tornados did you see in one day?

Did you sell your footage to a news programme? y/n

Did you get injured? y/n

If yes, what injury did you sustain?

Draw the devastation caused by the tornado you saw below:

How many miles did the tornado travel? m

Draw in the towns and buildings it ripped apart

At the same time you could complete these **Things To Do**
25: Capture the Moment in an Award-winning Photograph • 31: Experience Weightlessness • 53: Complete a Coast to Coast Road Trip Across America

Get a Piece of Art into an Exhibition

You've paid full price for your ticket. Finally you get to see the exhibition that has been advertised on TV, in newspapers and magazines to rave reviews, and it's been sold out since the opening day three months ago.

Within minutes of entering the gallery all the interest you originally had has long since disappeared, the fatigue caused by the sheer size of the show has reached your legs, causing MLS (Museum Leg Syndrome). Now you're looking for a bench rather than at the paintings but they're all full, taken up with the elderly and the bored. You've started to bypass whole rooms in search of a seat. You can see the coffee shop through the door. Face it, you're running for the exit.

Good art makes you want to own it, bad art inspires you to want to better it. So go on, stop procrastinating and start painting …

Common Exhibition Sayings

1. 'I Can Do Better Than That' 2. 'Did a Six-Year-Old Paint This?' 3. 'What Is It?' 4. 'I Love It' 5. 'I Hate It'

Subject Matter Make your work as controversial as possible; this way you'll generate huge amounts of publicity for yourself which could lead to more commissions, a newspaper column, a TV discussion show panellist, then obscurity (the Turner Prize).

Get a Piece of Art into an Exhibition **Form**

Once you have completed this **Thing To Do**, stick your Achieved Star here and fill in the form

Achieved

Opening date and time of the exhibition

d d m m y y y y :

Title of exhibition?

Where was the exhibition held?

What did you submit to the exhibition?

How long did your artwork take to produce?

Years Months Days

Was the exhibition part of a competition?

y/n If yes, did you win a prize? What was it?

What were the reviews for your work like?

Poor OK Good Very Good Excellent

Did you sell your work?

y/n If yes, how much did your work sell for? THINGS TO DO £/$

y/n Have you been commissioned to do more work?

y/n Have you been asked to submit anything into an exhibition since?

Attach a passport sized photograph of your exhibition piece here

45mm x 35mm

What was your work titled?

At the same time you could complete these **Things To Do**

03: Win an Award, Trophy or Prize • 10: Leave Your Mark in Graffiti • 63: Make the Front Page of a National Newspaper • 92: Own an Original Work of Art

101 Things To Do Before You Die
hello, my name is

Meet Someone With Your Own Name

Unless you have an incredibly unusual name, out of a population of 6 billion there has to be someone else out there with the same name as you.

You're out there somewhere. You're an actor, a doctor, a newborn baby all at the same time. You've seen your name at the end of movies, in the 'births, marriages and deaths' pages in the paper. These people are using your name to get ahead in their lives and careers. It's time you met up with them and had a word.

How to Find Yourself

- The internet is the best place to start. Type in your name and see who appears
- Try the phone book. Look in your local area first; you don't want to travel too far if you can help it
- Look at credits on a film – try to meet one of your more glamourous doppelgängers
- If there is no one with your name, either ask someone to legally change their name or be happy with the fact that there is no one in the world with the same name as you and celebrate the fact that you are truly unique

The World's Most Common Name
Mohammed is the most common first name and Chang is the most common surname, so if your name is Mohammed Chang you'll have no problem finding your namesake.

Meet Someone With Your Own Name **Form**

Once you have completed this **Thing To Do**, stick your Achieved Star here and fill in the form

Achieved

Date and time you met your doppelgänger

d d m m y y y y :

How did you find your doppelgänger?

Phone book · Movie credits · Word of mouth · Internet · Other

Where did you meet up?

What does your doppelgänger do for a living?

Where does your doppelgänger live?

Are you related?

y/n If yes, this is cheating. Please start this form again

Do you agree with the statements? Choose an answer from 1 to 5, 1 being the lowest and 5 being the highest. **Do you feel ...**

You got on well with each other? 1 2 3 4 5

That your doppelgänger liked you? 1 2 3 4 5

That you will become great friends? 1 2 3 4 5

Disappointed? 1 2 3 4 5

Do you think you'll meet up again?

y/n If no, why not?

At the same time you could complete these **Things To Do**
65: Shout 'Drinks Are on Me!' in a Pub or a Bar • 61: Get Away with the Perfect Practical Joke or Hoax • 94: Get Something Named After You

Ride the World's Biggest Rollercoasters

The queue for the rollercoaster snakes round and round for miles; you've joined the queue at a sign that says 'three hour wait from this sign', your friends ask 'Is it worth a three hour wait for a two minute ride?', you reply 'Hell yeah!'.

New rollercoasters are being built all the time, the fastest and longest ones are lucky to hold on to their record-breaking titles for a few years at the most. Approximately 50 new rollercoasters are built around the world every year, it's only a matter of time before the biggest and the best get even bigger. So, if you'd like to see your breakfast again and you like the feeling of your face being pulled apart by huge G-forces, this is the **Thing To Do** for you. Scour the world's amusement parks for the ultimate rollercoasters – and hold on tight.

Here are six of the world's fastest, tallest and longest rollercoasters to remind you what you had for dinner.

Record-breaking Rollercoasters

1. Top Thrill Dragster
Cedar Point, Ohio, USA

Fastest, 120mph, Tallest 420ft and Highest Drop, 400ft

2. Steel Dragon 2000
Nagashima Spa Land, Japan

World's Longest, 8,133ft

3. Colossus
Thorpe Park, Kent, England

Most Inversions, 10

4. Beast
Paramount's Kings Island, Ohio

Longest Wooden, 7,400ft

5. Leap the Dips
Lakemont Park, Altoona, Pennsylvania

World's Oldest, 1902

The Most Rollercoasters in One Place
Cedar Point Amusement Park in Ohio holds the record for an amusement park with the most rollercoasters in it. It has 16 in all.

Ride the World's Biggest Rollercoasters **Form**

Once you have completed this **Thing To Do**, stick your Achieved Star here and fill in the form

Achieved

Place a photo of you during the ride over the corresponding illustration and tick box when successfully completed

☐ Top Thrill Dragster
Cedar Point,
Ohio, USA

☐ Steel Dragon 2000
Nagashima Spa Land,
Japan

☐ Colossus
Thorpe Park,
Kent, England

☐ Superman the Escape
Six Flags Magic Mountain,
California, USA

☐ Incredible Hulk
Universal Studios Island of
Adventure, Orlando, Florida

☐ Son of the Beast
Paramount's Kings
Island, Ohio, USA

Which other rollercoasters have you ridden?

At the same time you could complete these **Things To Do**
16: Get into the *Guinness Book of World Records* • 21: Be a Human Guinea Pig • 25: Capture the Moment in an Award-winning Photograph

Stage Dive or Crowd Surf

Make the gig you're attending a more interactive experience. Stage dive at a Coldplay concert or crowd surf at a Radiohead gig, anything to liven those stiffs up a bit. Which will you do? Here are the choices:

Stage Diving

The act of jumping head first off the stage into the mosh pit below.

A lot easier to do before crushing disasters at festivals and tighter security controls. Make sure you pick a gig with a large crowd. A small crowd can quickly disperse, leaving you with no choice but a head-first clash with the floor. People in a big crowd can't move out the way, they have no choice but to catch you.

Crowd Surfing

The act of being passed over the top of the audience of a gig, usually in an arm-stretched-out-Jesus-on-the-cross pose.

Don't crowd surf right down to the front as the security guards will drag you out and send you back into the audience doldrums at the back. Ladies, make sure your T-shirt is tucked in, strangers' hands are prone to wandering.

Mosh Pit This is a tightly condensed area of the crowd at the very front of the stage. Moshing involves jumping and slamming around to music in cramped conditions. Do not fight against the flow of the mosh pit, beware of stage divers and crowd surfers from above.

Stage Dive or Crowd Surf **Form**

Once you have completed this **Thing To Do**,
stick your Achieved Star here and fill in the form

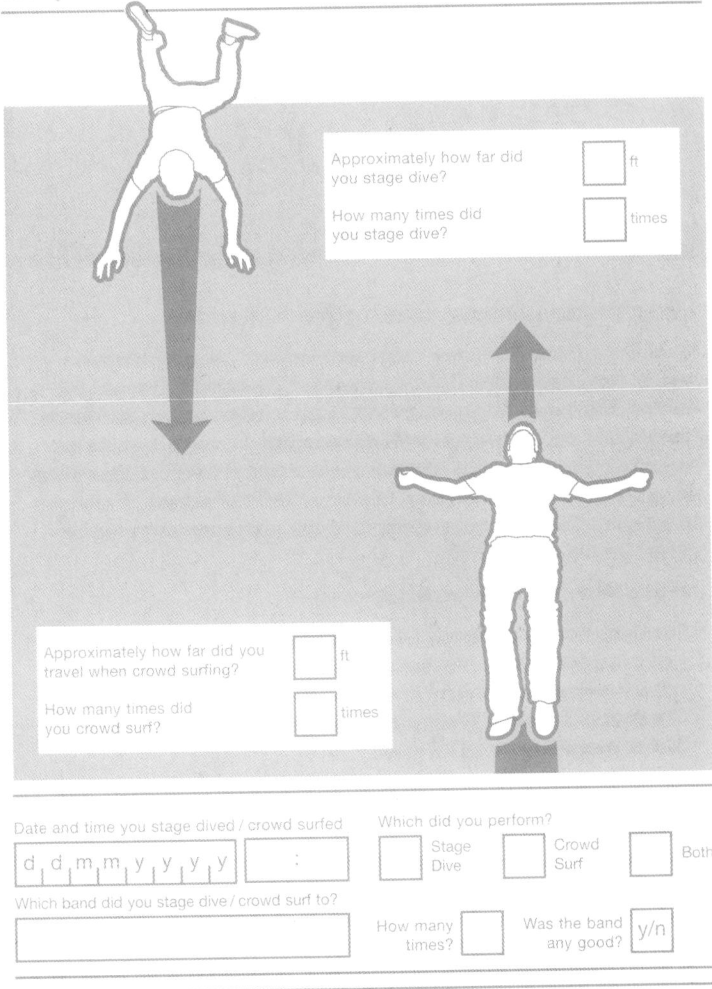

Approximately how far did you stage dive? ft

How many times did you stage dive? times

Approximately how far did you travel when crowd surfing? ft

How many times did you crowd surf? times

Date and time you stage dived / crowd surfed

d d m m y y y y :

Which did you perform?

Stage Dive | Crowd Surf | Both

Which band did you stage dive / crowd surf to?

How many times?

Was the band any good? y/n

At the same time you could complete these **Things To Do**
20: Get Backstage and Get Off with a Rock God •
23: Get Arrested • 29: Meet Your Idol • 71: Have Adventurous Sex

Get into the *Guinness Book of World Records*

Becoming a record breaker may take stamina (longest distance jumped on a pogo stick, **23.11 miles** in 12 hours 27 minutes by **Ashrita Furman**, USA), practice (Cream-cracker-eating, **Ambrose Mendy**, UK, ate 3 crackers in **49.15 seconds**) or maybe you could become a record breaker without even trying (World's tallest living person, **Radhouane Charbib**, Tunisia, at **7ft 8.9 inches**). There are thousands of records to attempt; just don't attempt anything too difficult or life-threatening.

So You Wanna Be a Record Breaker?

- Start your collection early: **Graham Barker**, Australia, who holds the record for the largest belly button fluff collection, started when he was a child and his collection is still growing
- Get lost in a crowd. The largest gathering of Santas stands at **3,618 people** in Taipei, Taiwan
- Break a record with the least amount of effort. The longest female beard stands at 27.9cm (11in); the record is held by **Vivian Wheeler**, USA
- Or cheat. Befriend someone at the world records office; get your new friend to paste your head onto the photograph of a record breaker's body; that way you can say you're in the *Guinness Book of World Records*

Record Breaker Procedure Contact *Guinness World Records* first before you attempt a record. If you break a record you will receive a certificate, although you might not make it into the book. Fill out the record attempt form on the website, **guinnessworldrecords.com**

Get into the *Guinness Book of World Records* **Form**

Once you have completed this **Thing To Do**, stick your Achieved Star here and fill in the form

Achieved

You're a Record Breaker

This is to certify that

Write your name here

Write the date you completed your record-breaking feat here

On

Write the details of your record-breaking feat here, including where, and how

This certificate is only a facsimile and cannot be used to prove your record-breaking feat

At the same time you could complete these **Things To Do**
03: Win an Award, Trophy or Prize • 05: Make a Discovery • 17: Own a Pointless Collection • 26: Bungee Jump • 28: Sky Dive • 46: Scuba Dive

Own a Pointless Collection

From Film Memorabilia to Weird Paraphernalia, Commemorative Plates to Contemporary Art, Marilyn Monroe to Mickey Mouse, or even Barbies to Belly Button Fluff, there are no limits to what you can collect. One person's junk is another person's prized possession.

In the past, it was a hands-on pastime of scouring charity shops and car boot sales to find the missing items to complete your collection. But now with the advent of the internet, and more importantly eBay, as long as you've got enough cash you can complete your collection by trawling around the world from the comfort of your own home. Just don't let your collection become an obsession.

If your collection has taken over, your obsessions can lead you into the cult of conventions – a dangerous world where socially rejected oddities and crazed forty-year-olds come to meet other obsessives. **Star Trek** conventions are where obsessed fans gather together dressed in their pyjamas, claim to be Klingons, and buy posters and plastic junk while speaking in a made-up language. Does this sound all too familiar?

Some Pointless Collections
Air Safety Cards • Fridge Magnets • Fake Masterpieces • Snowdomes • Beer Bottle Tops • Model Airplanes • Stamps • Egg Cups • Phone Cards • Key Rings • Garden Gnomes

Own a Pointless Collection **Form**

Once you have completed this **Thing To Do**, stick your Achieved Star here and fill in the form

Achieved

In which year did you start your collection?

Are you still collecting? y/n

Where do you get the majority of your collection from?

What does your collection consist of?

At what age did you start your collection?

Approximately how much is your collection worth? THINGS TO DO £/$

What made you start your collection?

What are your favourite pieces of your collection?

How many items do you have in your collection?

Is it a record-breaking collection? y/n

If no, has it ever been? y/n

Place a photo of your collection here

Bananas

Melons

Bananas BRAND BANANAS 1972 CELEBRATING 50 YEARS OF BANANAS

Euro Fruits

Pineapple Quality

Oranges SEVILLE PRODUCT OF SPAIN

BRAND

At the same time you could complete these **Things To Do**
16: Get into the *Guinness Book of World Records* • 25: Capture the Moment in an Award-winning Photograph • 75: Get a Tattoo and/or a Piercing

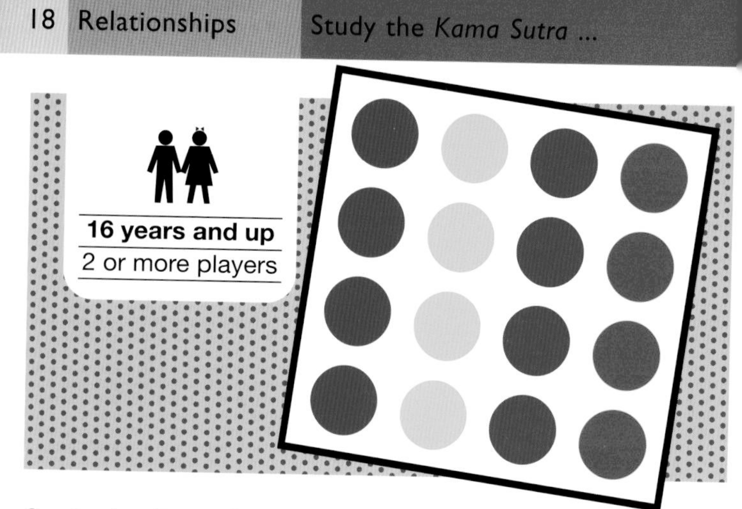

Study the *Kama Sutra* and Put Theory into Practice

Has your sex life gone off the boil or do you fancy a new challenge?

The *Kama Sutra* is the sex manual for amateur contortionists. A leg here, an arm there, it's more like Twister in the dark than a way of spicing up your bedroom moves. There are plenty of positions to master, and, with a bit of practice, imagination and a change of scenery, there's lots of potential for more to be invented. Here are nine for you to get your mind around, and your leg over.

Other Positions You've Tried
Position name here
Position name here
Position name here
Position name here
Position name here
Position name here
Position name here
Position name here
Position name here

Spice Up Your Life

- Pick a page number at random, turn to that page and attempt the position
- Clear the area immediately around you so you don't risk smashing anything (it could be dangerous if you're in a compromising position at the time)
- Stick to the floor, this way you haven't got far to fall

***Kama Sutra* History** The *Kama Sutra* was written approximately 1,500 years ago. *Kama* means desire; Kama is also the Hindu god of love. *Sutra* means rule or instruction. Only a fifth of the book is about sexual positions.

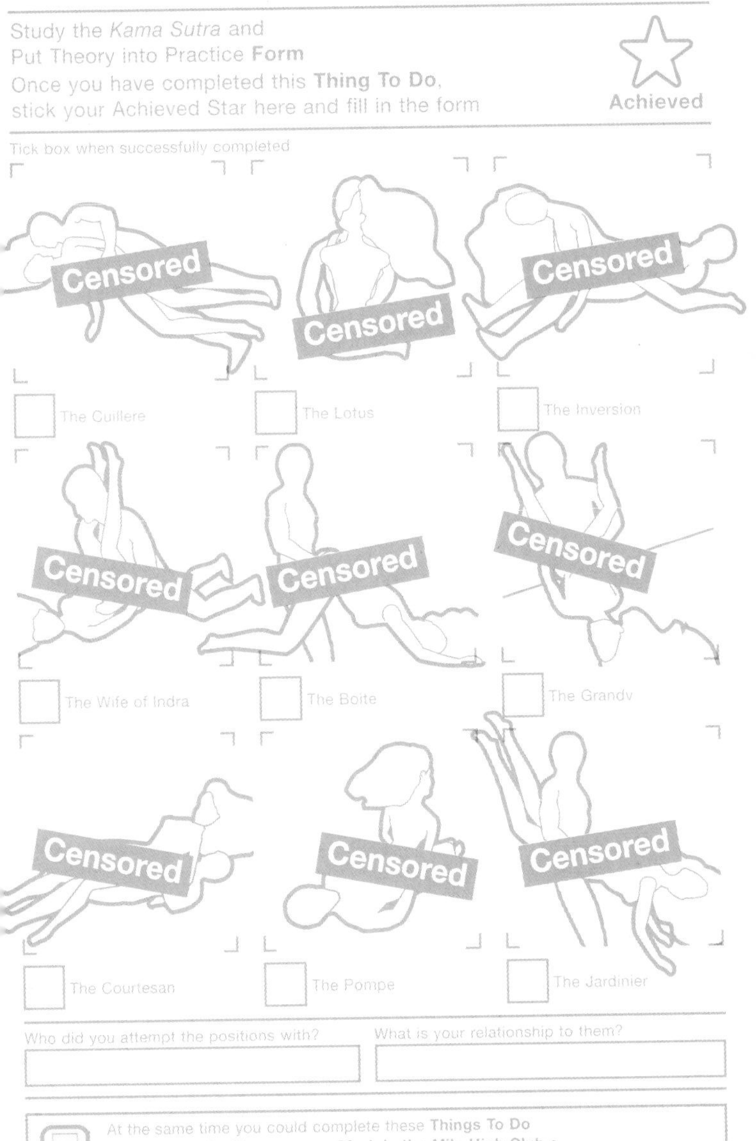

Study the *Kama Sutra* and
Put Theory into Practice **Form**
Once you have completed this **Thing To Do**,
stick your Achieved Star here and fill in the form

Achieved

Tick box when successfully completed

- [ ] The Cuillere
- [ ] The Lotus
- [ ] The Inversion
- [ ] The Wife of Indra
- [ ] The Boite
- [ ] The Grandv
- [ ] The Courtesan
- [ ] The Pompe
- [ ] The Jardinier

Who did you attempt the positions with?

What is your relationship to them?

At the same time you could complete these **Things To Do**
07: Be Part of a Threesome • 62: Join the Mile High Club • 71: Have Adventurous Sex • 101: Continue Your Gene Pool

Master Poker and Win Big in a Casino

Unreadable poker faces, bluffing and double bluffing. Poker is *the* card game, the only one worth mastering.

Practise your game either on the internet or sitting in dingy smoke-filled rooms. Work your way up to larger poker games in bigger smoke-filled rooms, playing against the best professional poker players in the country. All these years and years of practice will be needed for this **Thing To Do** even before you set one foot inside a casino, otherwise you'll get torn apart.

All you have are your skills, a hefty amount of bluffing and a certain amount of luck. Win, and winner takes all; get it wrong and you could lose everything. Whatever you do, if you win big, don't be tempted to stay. Keep your car keys in your pocket, your watch on your wrist and the shirt on your back.

It's not the taking part, it's the winning that counts.

Royal Flush
A, K, Q, J, 10
all of the same suit

Straight Flush
Any five card sequence
in the same suit

Four of a Kind
All four cards
of the same number

Full House
Three of a kind
combined with a pair

Flush
Any five cards of the same
suit, but not in sequence

Straight
Five cards in sequence,
but not in the same suit

Three of a Kind
Three cards of
the same number

Two Pair
Two separate pairs

Pair
Two cards of the
same number

The Ultimate Poker Tournament is considered to be the **World Series of Poker** tournament held every year at the Binion's Horseshoe Casino in Las Vegas. Anyone can enter as long as you have the $10,000 entry fee.

Master Poker and Win Big in a Casino **Form**

Once you have completed this **Thing To Do**, stick your Achieved Star here and fill in the form

Achieved

Date and time of your big win

d d m m y y y y :

Name of casino

Where is it?

How many people were you playing against?

In your view, how many were professional poker players?

Name the professional poker players below

Did you earn yourself a nickname?

y/n If yes, what was it?

Write, in the space provided, your winning hand; colour in the correct suit

What was your initial buy-in?

How much did you win?

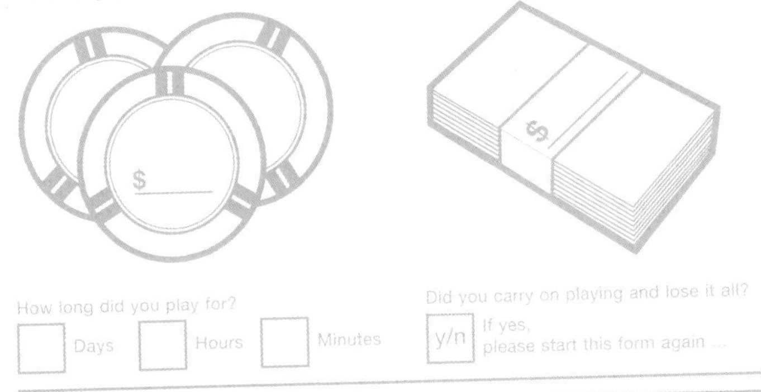

How long did you play for?

Days Hours Minutes

Did you carry on playing and lose it all?

y/n If yes, please start this form again ...

At the same time you could complete these **Things To Do**
30: Stay in the Best Suite in a Five Star Hotel • 65: Shout 'Drinks Are on Me!' in a Pub or a Bar • 72: Have Enough Money to Do All the Things on This List

Get Backstage and Get Off With a Rock God

It'll be something you'll boast about for years to come and it'll be the story you'll dine out on either because the rock star involved is über famous and no one will believe you, or the fact that they hardly make it onto the D-List and it was a hilarious fumble anyway. Get yourself into the forbidden backstage area, choose your target, gorge yourself on their drink and drugs and shamelessly throw yourself at them. If they're not having it, move on to the next member of the band. Always make the vocalist the first choice and end with the drummer.

We Will Rock You

- Become a roadie, handle their equipment and then manhandle the lead singer
- It's easier to get backstage at a big festival than a small gig. There are far more rock gods and godessess to choose from at a festival
- Make out you're a journalist
- Or just get straight to the point and do the groupie thing
- If you go back to their hotel room, trash it, throw the TV out the window and blame it on them
- Sell your story to a newspaper (see **Thing To Do** No. 63) and dish the dirt
- Get photographic evidence as proof of the event

Become a Roadie The typical roadie is an amateur rockstar with delusions of grandeur, hoping to make it big by hanging around with rock stars by setting up their musical equipment. Tattoos are essential. (For research, see *This is Spinal Tap*)

Get Backstage and Get Off With a Rock God **Form**

Once you have completed this **Thing To Do**, stick your Achieved Star here and fill in the form

Achieved

Get Backstage

Date you got backstage

d d m m y y y y

Which gig were you at?

How did you get backstage?

With a wristband | You conned your way | Claimed to be someone else | You snuck in

You're a roadie | You're in the band | You're in a band | Other

If other, please specify

Which famous people did you see backstage?

Get off with a Rock God

Date you got off with a rock god

d d m m y y y y

Who was it?

What is their role in the band?

Which band are they in?

Is the band any good?

Amazing | Brilliant | OK | So-so | Rubbish

What did you get up to?

... or Someone Famous

Date you got off with them

d d m m y y y y

Who was it?

Why are they famous?

Is the celebrity ...

A List? | B List? | C List? | D List? | Lower than D?

What did you get up to?

Heckling

Name the most famous people you've heckled

At the same time you could complete these **Things To Do**

07: Be Part of a Threesome • 71: Have Adventurous Sex • 101: Continue Your Gene Pool

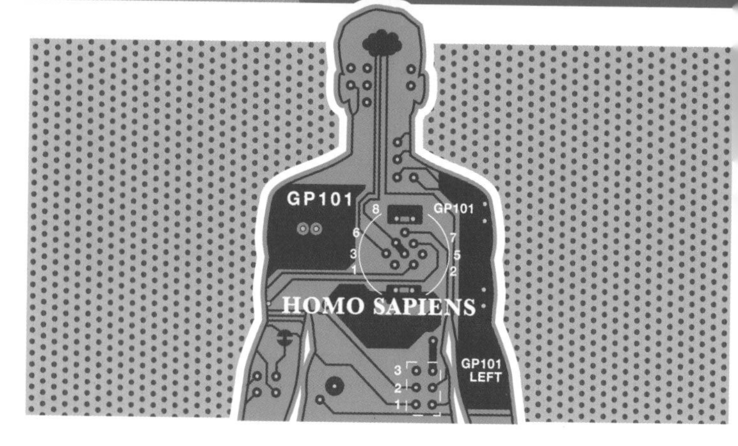

Be a Human Guinea Pig

If it wasn't for brave members of the general public we wouldn't have vaccines for life-threatening diseases. If you're going to do something worthwhile with your life do this one thing; in the long run you could help millions of people from the results of the tests on you. It's also a great way to try out the latest drugs; just try not to get given the placebo.

How to become a Human Guinea Pig

- Universities are keen to run experiments on poor, strapped-for-cash students. You can be electrocuted, deprived of sleep, force-fed and subjected to numerous psychological tests in exchange for a little beer money. Also try the pharmaceutical companies and hospitals
- The experiment could be anything from a questionnaire to an experimental drug treatment course. Some experiments can be over in an afternoon, others can run for years. Make sure you know what you're getting yourself into before you sign up
- Look on the internet for human guinea pig advertisements, but don't answer any German adverts featuring cannibalism

Self-experimentation When conducting experiments on yourself make sure you have a helper present just in case your experiment goes spectacularly wrong; they can call the emergency services on your behalf.

Be a Human Guinea Pig **Form**

Once you have completed this **Thing To Do**, stick your Achieved Star here and fill in the form

Achieved

Date your clinical trial started
d d m m y y y y

Date your clinical trial ended
d d m m y y y y

Name of experiment

Pills

What is the name of the drug?

Did you have to take drugs daily? y/n

How many weeks did you have to take them?

Write the amount of pills you had to take daily, on the pill box

S	M	T	W	T	F	S

What type of pills did you have to take? Tick the correct shape

Were there any side effects? y/n

If yes, list the side effects

Were you given the placebo drugs? y/n

Psychological

What type of test was it?

What did you learn about yourself?

Physical

Were electrodes used? If yes, draw on the figures below where the electrodes were placed

Female Back

Male Back

Female Front

Male Front

Outcome

Were your results helpful to them? y/n

Were they helpful to you? y/n

Are you glad it's over? y/n

Would you do it again? y/n

At the same time you could complete these **Things To Do**
05: Make a Discovery • 87: Conquer Your Fear • 94: Get Something Named After You

Go Up in a Hot Air Balloon

Up, Up and Away

A great way to go on safari. A relaxing and silent way to hunt the animals with your high-powered assault camera, but if this isn't exciting enough ...

Up, Up and Bombs Away

At present, the record for the highest balloon flight stands at 102,800ft, set in August 1960 by Colonel Joseph Kittinger, followed seconds later by his record for the world's highest sky dive, both of which have stood for over forty years.

Around the World

Balloon flight doesn't have to be slow. Various attempts at travelling round the world in a hot air balloon have taken place; to do this you need speed. To achieve high speeds you need to catch fast-flowing streams of air. High up in the atmosphere, these can propel you to speeds of around 140mph.

For a diagram of the highest balloon flight to date, see **Thing To Do** No. 90.

The First Successful Nonstop Around the World Balloon Flight On 21 March 1999, after 19 days, 21 hours and 55 minutes, Bertrand Piccard and Brian Jones landed in the Egyptian desert after flying 28,431 miles since they took off from the Swiss Alps.

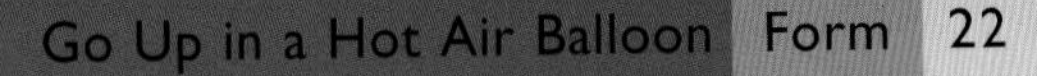

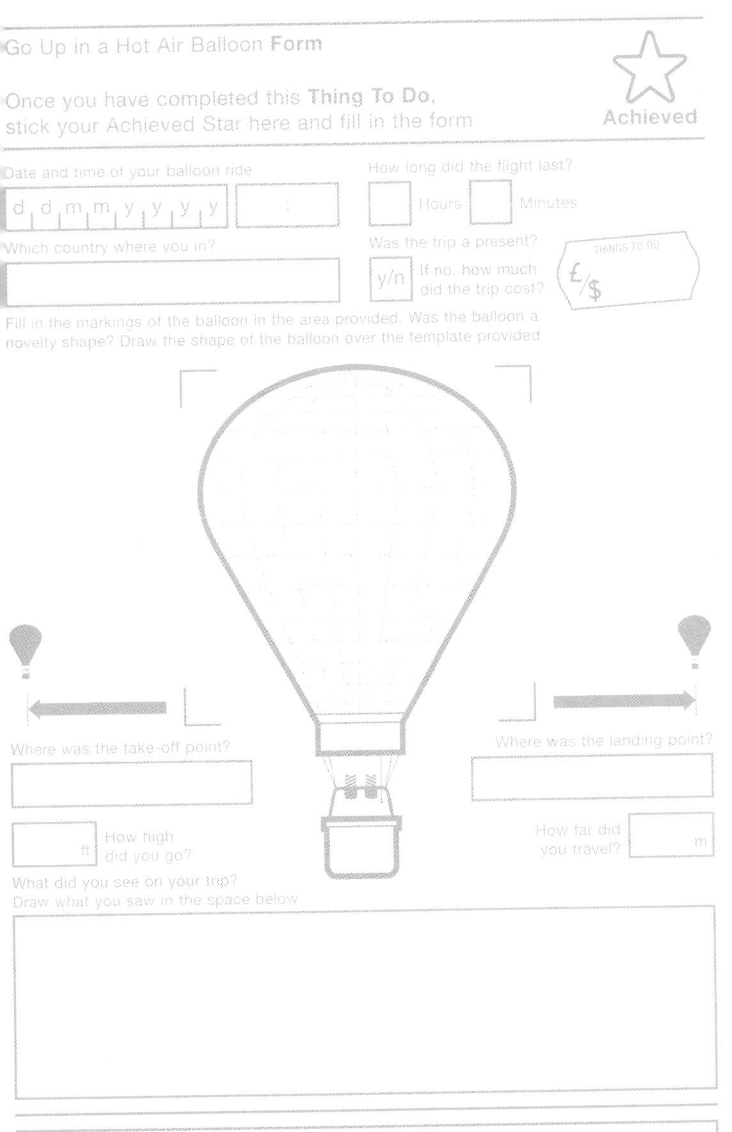

Go Up in a Hot Air Balloon **Form**

Once you have completed this **Thing To Do**,
stick your Achieved Star here and fill in the form

Achieved

Date and time of your balloon ride

d d m m y y y y :

How long did the flight last?

Hours Minutes

Which country where you in?

Was the trip a present?

y/n If no, how much did the trip cost?

THINGS TO DO £/$

Fill in the markings of the balloon in the area provided. Was the balloon a novelty shape? Draw the shape of the balloon over the template provided

Where was the take-off point?

Where was the landing point?

ft How high did you go?

How far did you travel? m

What did you see on your trip?
Draw what you saw in the space below

At the same time you could complete these **Things To Do**
26: Bungee Jump • 38: See These Animals in the Wild ... • 43: Throw a Dart into a Map and Travel to Where it Lands • 88: Get Married Unusually

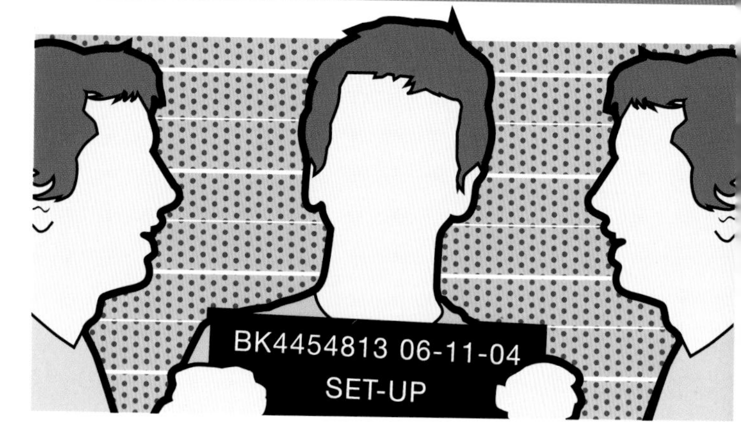

Get Arrested

This is the easiest **Thing To Do** on the whole list. For a start you could get arrested while attempting one of the other **Things To Do**, for example attempting anything from the Have Adventurous Sex page could lead to an arrest for indecent exposure. (see **Thing To Do** No. 71). Let's face it, it doesn't even have to be anything to do with this book, there are plenty of other ways to get yourself arrested. It doesn't even have to be anything major; there are some very petty crimes out there.

I Fought the Law

- In the borough of Westminster, London, it is illegal to dance in a public house
- In California, it is illegal to drive more than two thousand sheep down Hollywood Boulevard at one time
- In Miami it is illegal for a man to be seen publicly in a strapless gown
- No one may catch a fish with his bare hands in Kansas
- In Alabama, it is illegal to wear a fake moustache that causes laughter in a church
- In Tulsa, Oklahoma, it is against the law to open a soda bottle without the supervision of a licensed engineer
- In Seattle, Washington, it is illegal to carry a concealed weapon that is over six feet in length

---

Get Out of Jail Free The 'get out of jail free' card in Monopoly doesn't work in real life. The card has been produced during various court cases in the past, but so far it hasn't worked. At least they took a chance.

Get Arrested **Form**

Once you have completed this **Thing To Do**, stick your Achieved Star here and fill in the form

Achieved

Date and time of your arrest

d d m m y y y y :

Where were you when you were arrested?

What were you doing at the time?

Was it a wrongful arrest? y/n

If yes, why shouldn't you have been arrested?

Were handcuffs used? y/n

Were you bundled into a van? y/n

Place your mugshot photographs here

How long were you in the cells for? Hours

Were you drunk? y/n

Did you have to share a cell? y/n

If yes, who with?

Were you a victim of police brutality? y/n

Did you provoke them? y/n

Were you charged with anything? y/n

If yes, what were you charged with?

At the same time you could complete these **Things To Do**

04: Catch a Fish With Your Bare Hands • 10: Leave Your Mark in Graffiti • 71: Have Adventurous Sex • 83: Skinny Dip at Midnight

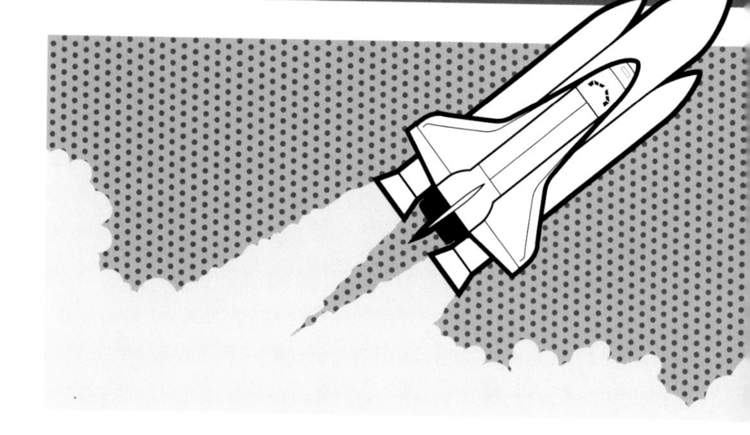

See a Space Shuttle Launch

Since Yuri Gagarin became the first person in space with the first manned flight on 12 April 1961, only 450 people have travelled into space since, and of those 450 people, only 12 have walked on the moon.

If your childhood dream was to become an astronaut (see **Thing To Do** No. 8) the odds are heavily stacked against you. Even if you did finally become an astronaut after years of hard work and long hours, there is no guarantee that you will get picked for a mission into space. Face it, the only way you're likely to get into space is via the X prize.

The words 'one day I'll make it into space' seem a bit hollow now; let's stick to watching the Space Shuttle take off instead.

Space Shuttle Facts

The original Shuttle fleet consisted of six craft, *Enterprise*, *Columbia*, *Challenger*, *Discovery*, *Atlantis* and *Endeavour*

The Space Shuttle programme began on 12 April 1981, exactly twenty years to the day after Yuri Gagarin's first manned space flight

It takes NASA three months to prepare for a launch

At launch, a Shuttle contains more than one million pounds of propellant

Each Shuttle launch costs at least $400 million

In orbit, the Shuttle travels at 17,500 miles an hour

During re-entry, the Shuttle's thermal tiles heat to over 3,000 degrees Fahrenheit. Inside the vehicle, the temperature is constant at 70 degrees

What is the X Prize? The X prize is a competition with a prize of $10,000,000 to the first team that can finance, build and launch their own spacecraft over 60 miles into space, return back to earth and repeat the launch with the same craft within two weeks.

See a Space Shuttle Launch **Form**

Once you have completed this **Thing To Do**, stick your Achieved Star here and fill in the form

Achieved

Scheduled date and time of the launch

d d m m y y y y :

Flight number

Which shuttle was used?

What was the reason for the mission?

Did the launch take off on time?

y/n If no, how long was the launch delayed for?

Days Hours Mins

What was the reason for the delay?

Did you manage to see the relaunch?

y/n If no, why not? Write your reasons below

There were [ ] astronauts involved in the mission

Their names were ...

How many days did the mission last?

Did you get to see inside the ...

Space Shuttle? y/n Command centre? y/n

How close were you to the launch?

m

At the same time you could complete these **Things To Do**

08: Realise Your Childhood Dream • 31: Experience Weightlessness • 72: Have Enough Money to Do All the Things on This List • 90: Join the 16-Mile High Club

Capture the Moment in an Award-winning Photograph

Cameras are part of our everyday lives. They're everywhere, you can't escape them. They're on our streets to catch us speeding, on the buildings to watch us behaving badly, in the shops and in our phones. Big Brother is watching you every second. There was a time when you'd hear the line 'I wish I had my camera with me'; now you can't escape the damn things. You now have no excuse not to catch the moment.

At one time or another, you must have collected your photographs from the developers to find quality control advice stickers stuck across the faces of your nearest and dearest that read 'This photo is too dark' and 'Do not photograph your subjects in front of bright light' written on them; the sticker might as well have read 'This photo is rubbish'. Time to heed their advice and take the perfect photos.

Life Through a Lens

- Carry your camera everywhere with you. If you've left it at home, go back and get it. You never know when the prize-winning moment is going to occur
- Always have plenty of film handy; you don't want to run out of film during a world-changing event. If your camera is digital, make sure the battery is fully charged

Lomo Photography Rules 1. Take your Lomo everywhere you go 2. Use it anytime 3. Lomography is not an interference with your life but a part of it 4. Get as close as possible to the objects of your lomographic desire 5. Don't think 6. Be fast 7. You don't have to know beforehand what is on your film 8. Nor afterwards 9. Try the shot from the hip 10. Don't worry about (golden) rules

Capture the Moment in an Award-winning Photograph **Form**

Once you have completed this **Thing To Do**, stick your Achieved Star here and fill in the form

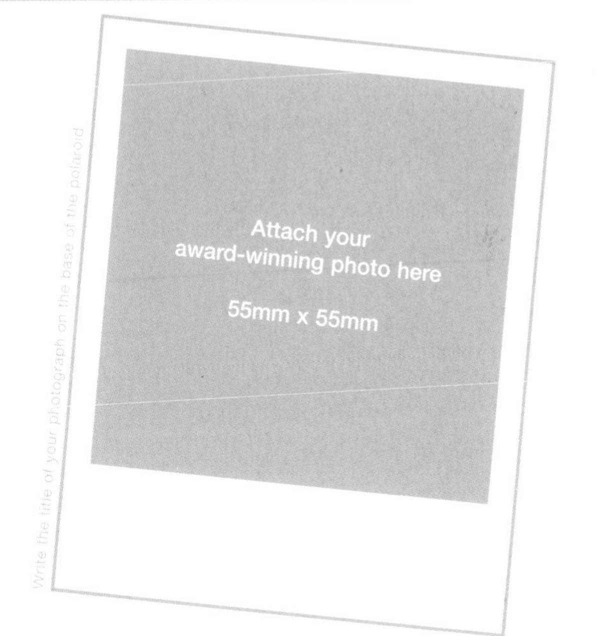

Attach your award-winning photo here
55mm x 55mm
Write the title of your photograph on the base of the polaroid

Date and time of the photograph

d d m m y y y y :

Date and time of the private view

d d m m y y y y :

What was the name of the competition?

How many entrants were there?

Did you think you had a good chance of winning? y/n

Which position did your photograph achieve?

1st 2nd 3rd Other

Was there prize money? If yes, how much did you win? THINGS TO DO £/$

Did someone buy your work? If yes, how much for? THINGS TO DO £/$

If the prize wasn't monetary, what was it?

At the same time you could complete these **Things To Do**

11: Storm Chase a Tornado • 27: See an Erupting Volcano • 63: Make the Front Page of a National Newspaper • 98: Go on a Demonstration

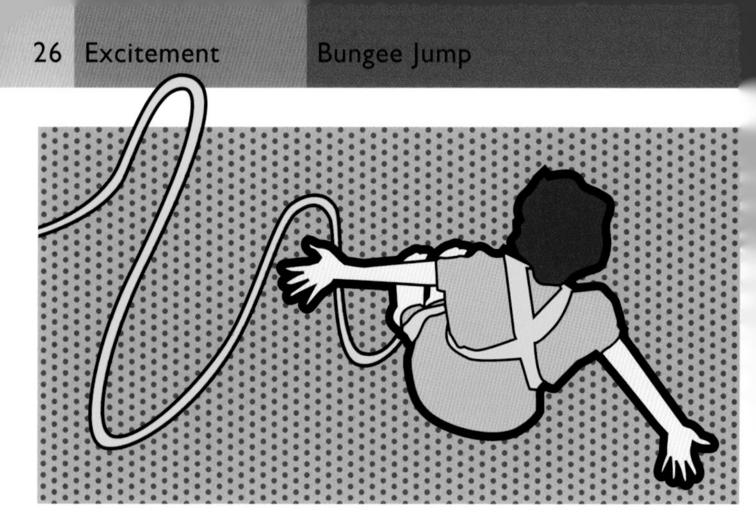

Bungee Jump

Throwing yourself head first off a bridge isn't usual behaviour, it's either suicide or insanity, but it's a totally different matter if you have an enormous elastic band tied around your legs.

If you're into extreme sports this is probably the first thing you will do – a death-defying leap over a fast-flowing river on a elastic band – but if you haven't jumped yet and you're looking for the ideal place to do it you might as well go for one of the highest. At 700ft, the bridge over the Bloukrans river in South Africa boasts the world's largest commercial bridge bungee jump. Rather than trekking for hours down to the riverside, it's a great way to see the river close up, and then from far away and then close up again ...

Don't Stop Me Now

- If 700ft is still not high enough you could always bungee jump from a building, a helicopter or a hot air balloon. With a hot air balloon you can bungee jump from as high as you dare go. Mind you, the only way down after that is to sky dive. Two extreme sports for the price of one

The Birth of Modern Bungee Jumping
In 1979, Alan Weston, David Kirke, Tim Hunt, and Simon Keeling were the first four people to bungee jump; they jumped from the Clifton Suspension Bridge in Bristol.

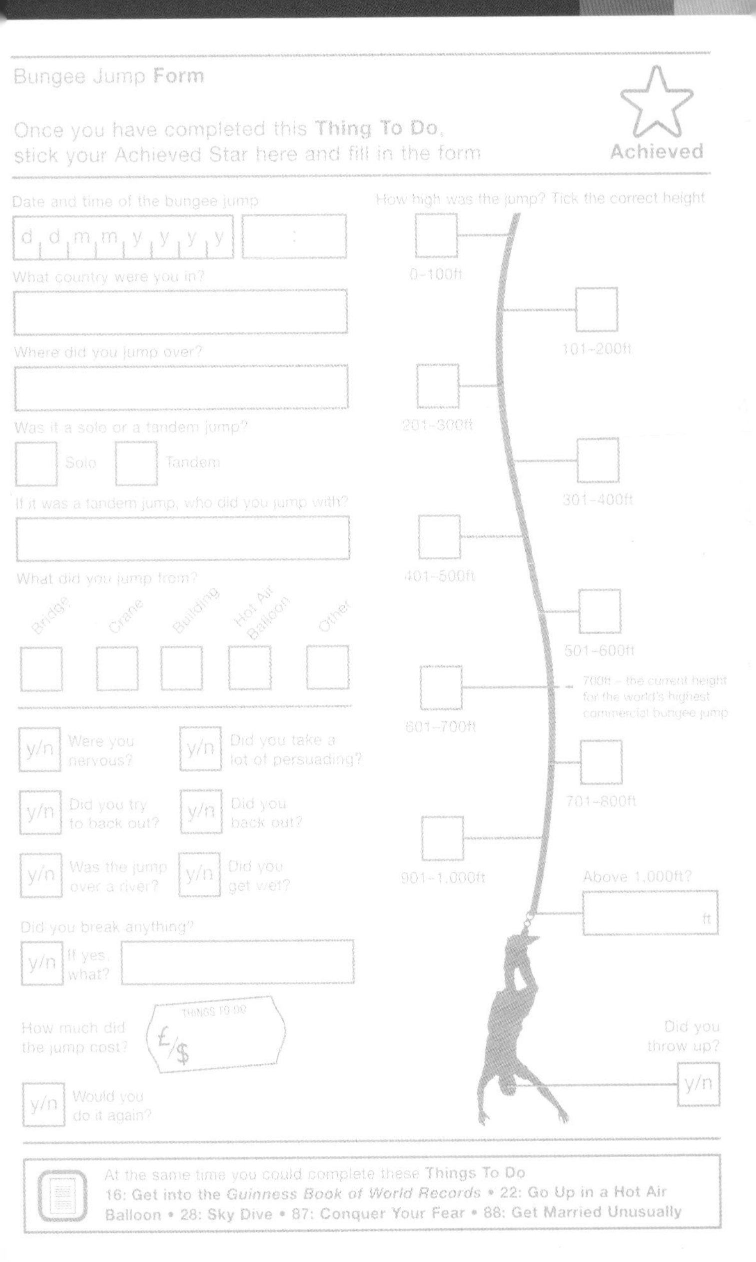
Bungee Jump **Form**

Once you have completed this **Thing To Do**, stick your Achieved Star here and fill in the form

Achieved

Date and time of the bungee jump

d d m m y y y y :

What country were you in?

Where did you jump over?

Was it a solo or a tandem jump?

Solo Tandem

If it was a tandem jump, who did you jump with?

What did you jump from?

Bridge Crane Building Hot Air Balloon Other

y/n Were you nervous?

y/n Did you take a lot of persuading?

y/n Did you try to back out?

y/n Did you back out?

y/n Was the jump over a river?

y/n Did you get wet?

Did you break anything?

y/n If yes, what?

How much did the jump cost? THINGS TO DO £/$

y/n Would you do it again?

How high was the jump? Tick the correct height

0–100ft

101–200ft

201–300ft

301–400ft

401–500ft

501–600ft

700ft – the current height for the world's highest commercial bungee jump

601–700ft

701–800ft

901–1,000ft

Above 1,000ft? ft

Did you throw up? y/n

At the same time you could complete these **Things To Do**
16: Get into the *Guinness Book of World Records* • 22: Go Up in a Hot Air Balloon • 28: Sky Dive • 87: Conquer Your Fear • 88: Get Married Unusually

See an Erupting Volcano

Being in the right place at the right time to see a volcano erupt is usually down to either chance, scientific study or pure bad luck.

The people of Pompeii knew all about being in the right place at the wrong time; they got to see a spectacular fire and light show but weren't around to see the finale.

The World's Most Active Volcano

For the best chance of seeing some first class volcanic action, Mount Etna is the place to be. Situated in East Sicily, and standing over 3,300ft high, it has the title of being the world's most active volcano; it has been in a state of constant activity for over 3,500 years.

It's Getting Hot in Here

- The temperature of lava can be different from volcano to volcano. The lava from one could be 200°C while it could be 1,250°C from another

The World's Most Active Volcanos

Etna, Sicily
Over 3,500 years

Stromboli, Italy
Over 2,000 years

Yasur, Vanuatu
Over 800 years

Piton de la Fournaise, Réunion
Since 1920

Santa Maria, Guatemala
Since 1922

Dukono, Indonesia
Since 1933

Sangay, Ecuador
Since 1934

Ambrym, Vanuatu
Since 1935

Suwanose-jima, Japan
Since 1949

Tinakula, Solomon Islands
Since 1951

Mount Etna
The height of Mount Etna fluctuates due to the frequent eruptions constantly changing its height. Its height fluctuates around 3,340m (10,958ft).

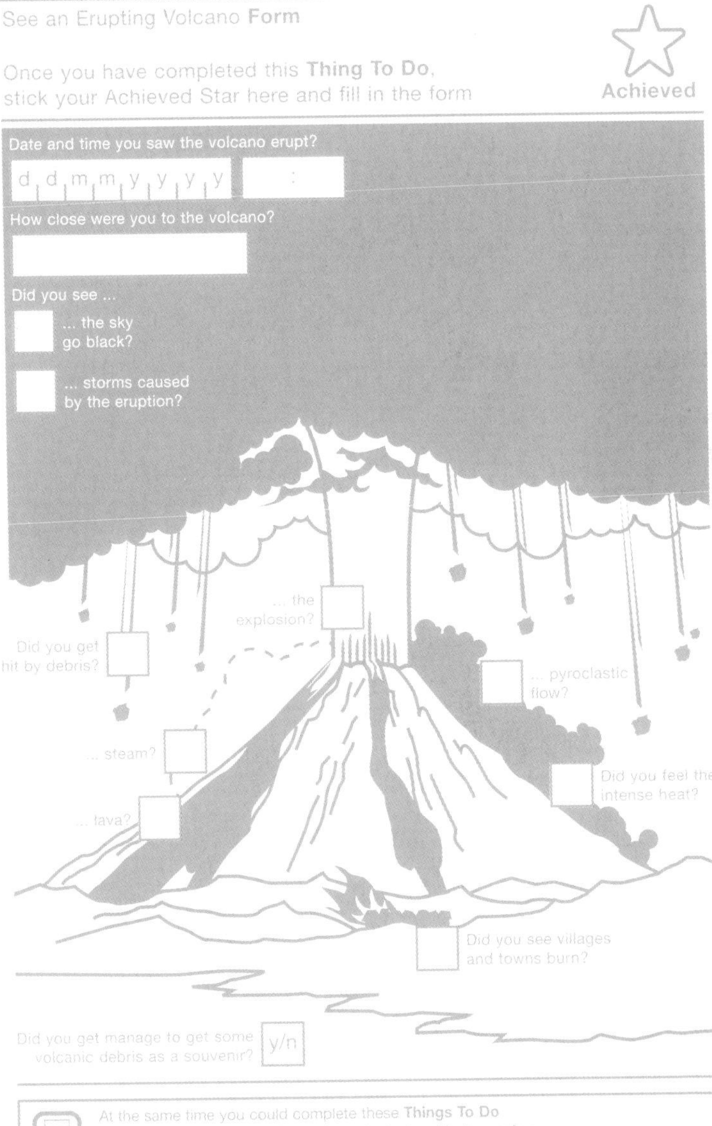

See an Erupting Volcano Form
Once you have completed this Thing To Do, stick your Achieved Star here and fill in the form
Achieved
Date and time you saw the volcano erupt?
d d m m y y y y
:
How close were you to the volcano?
Did you see ...
... the sky go black?
... storms caused by the eruption?
... the explosion?
Did you get hit by debris?
... pyroclastic flow?
... steam?
Did you feel the intense heat?
... lava?
Did you see villages and towns burn?
Did you get manage to get some volcanic debris as a souvenir?
y/n

At the same time you could complete these **Things To Do**
25: Capture the Moment in an Award-winning Photograph • 69: In Various Languages, Learn to Say ... • 87: Conquer Your Fear

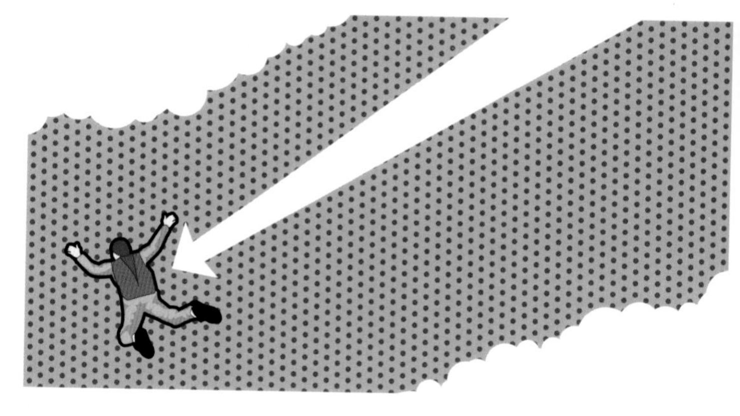

Sky Dive

You might need a hand, or rather a shove to complete this **Thing To Do**. If you don't trust yourself to pull the cord at the right time or fall the right way up you can do a tandem jump; this is when you are harnessed to a professional skydiver and you can put your life into their hands. Or you can take your life in your own hands and sky dive solo. Depending on the height you jump from, a skydive can be from 30 to 60 seconds of freefalling and then another 4 to 7 minutes of parachuting. You can also expect to fall at an average of 120mph.

It might be a daunting prospect but once you've jumped you'll want to do it again and again. And once you've mastered the art of sky-diving think of the benefits; you can use your new skills to descend into the Glastonbury festival for free – it gives a whole new meaning to jumping the fence. Once you've landed, cover yourself head to toe in mud and turn your parachute into a tent.

For a diagram of the highest sky dive to date see **Thing To Do** No. 90.

Highest sky dive Set in August 1960 by Colonel Joseph Kittinger, the balloon he jumped from reached 102,800ft. He fell 16 miles (84,700ft) in 4 minutes and 37 seconds at a speed of 714mph, faster than the speed of sound, before his parachute opened.

Sky Dive **Form**

Once you have completed this **Thing To Do**, stick your Achieved Star here and fill in the form

Achieved

Date and time of your sky dive

d d m m y y y y :

What country were you in?

Where did you jump?

How long did you train for?

Days Hours Minutes

Was it a solo or a tandem jump?

Solo Tandem

If it was a tandem jump, who did you jump with?

Height of jump

ft

How much did it cost?

Approximately how many seconds did you freefall for?

How low did you get before you opened your parachute?

ft

y/n Were you nervous?

y/n Did you try to back out?

y/n Did you take a lot of persuading?

y/n Did you back out?

How much did it cost? THINGS TO DO £/$

Did the parachute open correctly? y/n

If no, did you have to use your reserve parachute? y/n

What was the top speed you reached?

mph

Did you throw up? y/n

Approximately how long did the jump last?

Did you land correctly?

y/n If no, did you break anything?

Would you ever do it again? y/n

At the same time you could complete these **Things To Do**
16: Get into the *Guinness Book of World Records* • 22: Go Up in a Hot Air Balloon • 87: Conquer Your Fear • 88: Get Married Unusually

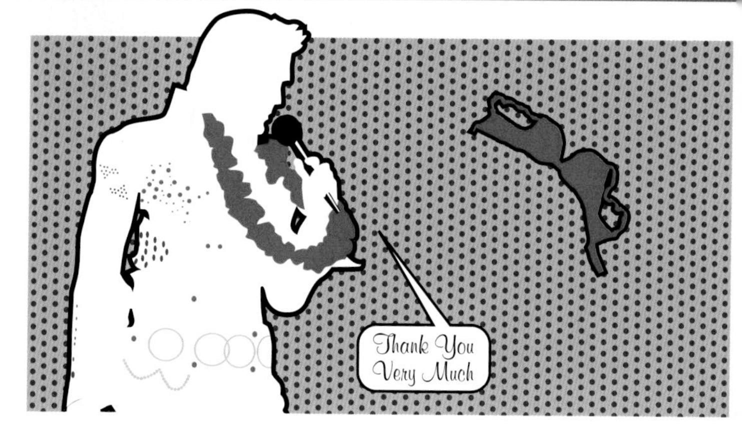

Meet Your Idol

You've been hiding in the bushes of their house for over two days and you've been through the bins to see what they've had for dinner. They haven't been answering your calls for weeks and you haven't seen them wearing the jumper you knitted for them with love hearts and your face on it. Being a celebrity stalker is not the best way to meet your idol.

If you find that every square inch of wall space in your bedroom has your idol's face on it, you're dressing in the same clothes as them and you have their phone number, you're one step away from a restraining order.

Proof You Met Your Idol

- Get an autograph
- Get a photograph of you and your idol together
- Try to encourage them to give you one of their personal possessions
- Repay their kindness – invite them to dinner

See the Final Resting Places of

Marilyn Monroe
Westwood Village Memorial Park
Westwood, California

James Dean
Park Cemetery
Fairmount, Indiana

Jim Morrison
Père-Lachaise Cemetery, Paris

Elvis Presley
Graceland Mansion
3734 Elvis Presley Blvd
Memphis, Tennessee

Kurt Cobain
Allegedly, one third of Kurt's ashes are in a Buddhist temple in New York, one third in the Wishkah River and the other third are still with Courtney Love

When You Meet Your Idol Get your idol to sign your breasts or another intimate part of your body, get them to phone your mother for a chat, get them to autograph the painting you've done of them and show them photographs of your shrine.

Meet Your Idol **Form**

Once you have completed this **Thing To Do**, stick your Achieved Star here and fill in the form

Achieved

Place the photograph of you and your idol below. Either place your faces over the ones provided or place the whole picture in the space below

Date you met your idol

d d m m y y y y

How long were you with them?

Days Hours Mins

Are you friends since you meet? y/n

You're not a stalker, are you? y/n

Who is your idol?

Did you get an autograph? y/n

Did you get anything else from them?

If you are a stalker ...

Do you have a restraining order against you? y/n

Where did you meet him/her?

If you did, list the items below

Have you met up since? y/n

Did he/she remember you? y/n

At the same time you could complete these **Things To Do**
20: Get Backstage and Get Off with a Rock God • 30: Stay in the Best Suite in a Five Star Hotel • 71: Have Adventurous Sex • 78: Drink a Vintage Wine

Stay in the Best Suite in a Five Star Hotel

Staying in a hotel room on holiday is a means to an end. You're out exploring all day, hardly spending any time in the hotel, and when you are in your room, you're asleep.

Hotels are too expensive for the service they offer. You pay good money and you expect a decent room with the basics. What you get is a room that overlooks the car park, wallpaper that looks as if it's been there since the turn of the century, an uncomfortable bed, no hot water, one complimentary biscuit and three used tea bags. Once in a while you should treat yourself to a decent room in a top class hotel, where you're pampered from the moment you walk in until the moment you leave.

Your Room

- Make sure your suite has got everything you need, and plenty of other things that you don't. Book for a whole weekend, and don't leave the room until you check out
- If you do use the mini bar, save yourself a huge addition to your bill by replacing the missing items with the exact same drink from the local shops
- Stealing the towels, dressing gown and soaps is compulsory

The Most Expensive Hotel Room
The Imperial Suite in the President Wilson Hotel in Geneva, Switzerland. The cost of the room per night is just under £21,000 / $40,000.

Stay in the Best Suite in a Five Star Hotel **Form**

Once you have completed this **Thing To Do**,
stick your Achieved Star here and fill in the form

Achieved

Date and time of your stay

d d m m y y y y :

How much did the room cost per night? THINGS TO DO £/$

What was the name of hotel you stayed in?

Did you pay? If you didn't, who did?

Which country were you in?

Did you stay in a penthouse? y/n

What was the name of the suite you stayed in?

How many rooms did your suite have?

Were the staff extremely nice to you? y/n

What did the amazing views consist of?

Did you leave the suite at all during your stay? y/n

Did you steal the towels and complimentary soaps? y/n

Draw in the space provided your room and all the extras it came with

Did your suite have ...

A valet/concierge?

A Jacuzzi?

A swimming pool?

A private bar?

A private cinema?

A conference room?

A dining room?

A four-poster bed?

A kitchen?

An office?

A masterpiece?

A private elevator?

At the same time you could complete these **Things To Do**
54: Make at Least One Huge Purchase You Can't Afford • 71: Have Adventurous Sex • 72: Have Enough Money to Do All the Things on This List

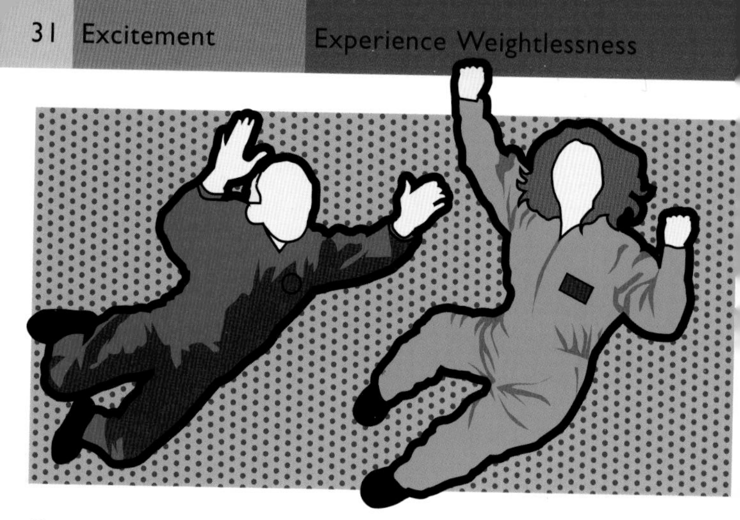

Experience Weightlessness

There are three ways of achieving weightlessness: the first is to take a flight into outer space; the second is in the zero gravity plane used by NASA and the Russian Space Agency to expose their astronauts to the effects of weightlessness.

Think of an aeroplane cabin without any seats, windows or furnishings of any kind, an interior covered in plate metal; this is exactly what the zero g plane looks like inside: a huge long space for astronauts to practise working in weightless conditions. The other main difference is the way they fly it.

The plane climbs at an angle of 45° from 24,000 to 32,000 feet then the plane is allowed to free fall for 20–30 seconds, causing the weightlessness felt by the astronauts. The plane then goes into a 30° dive back down to 24,000 feet before starting the process over again.

If you have a fear of flying there is no way you'll be able to do this **Thing To Do**. Another consideration is the cost – to experience the zero g plane it costs approximately $5,500, so start saving for your ride on the Vomit Comet.

There is a third and free way to become weightless – inside a falling elevator – this way is definitely not recommended.

What is Weightlessness? Weightlessness is the appearance of being lighter than air but it is in fact a state of freefalling. You, and everything around you, are falling at the same rate but the effects of the Earth's gravity are holding you in place. A more correct term for this state is microgravity.

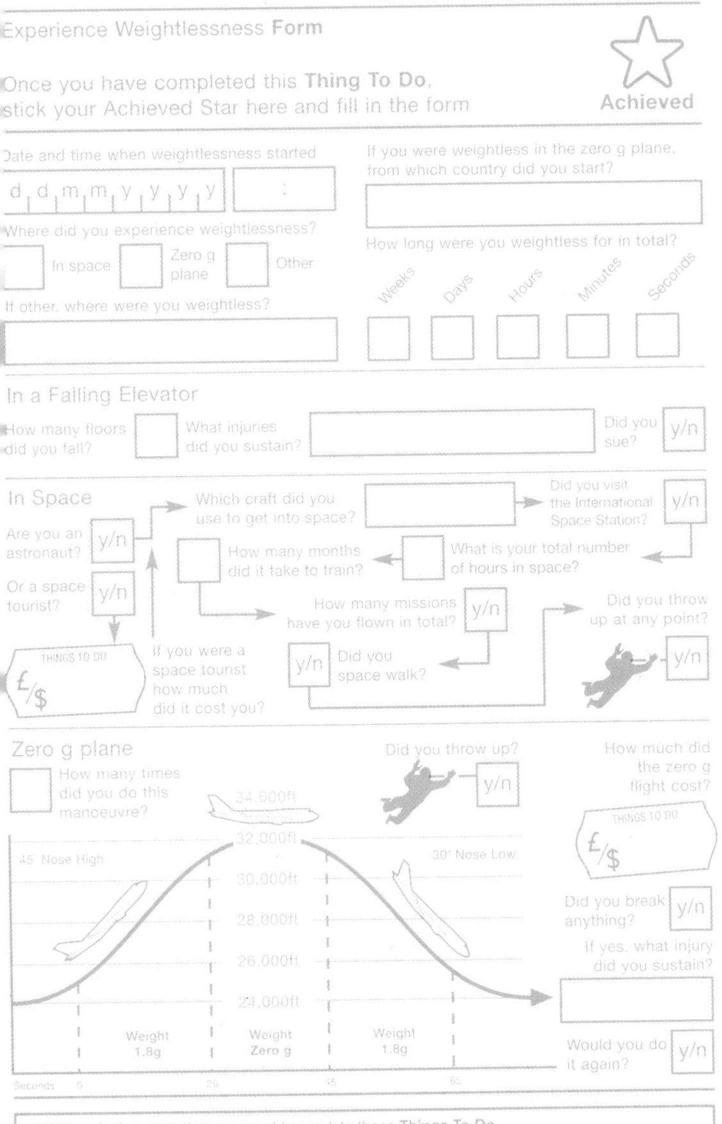

Experience Weightlessness Form
Once you have completed this Thing To Do, stick your Achieved Star here and fill in the form
Achieved
Date and time when weightlessness started
d d m m y y y y
:
If you were weightless in the zero g plane, from which country did you start?
Where did you experience weightlessness?
In space
Zero g plane
Other
How long were you weightless for in total?
Weeks
Days
Hours
Minutes
Seconds
If other, where were you weightless?
In a Falling Elevator
How many floors did you fall?
What injuries did you sustain?
Did you sue?
y/n
In Space
Are you an astronaut?
y/n
Or a space tourist?
y/n
Which craft did you use to get into space?
Did you visit the International Space Station?
y/n
What is your total number of hours in space?
How many months did it take to train?
How many missions have you flown in total?
y/n
Did you throw up at any point?
y/n
Did you space walk?
y/n
THINGS TO DO
£/$
If you were a space tourist how much did it cost you?
Zero g plane
How many times did you do this manoeuvre?
Did you throw up?
y/n
How much did the zero g flight cost?
THINGS TO DO
£/$
34,000ft
32,000ft
30,000ft
28,000ft
26,000ft
24,000ft
45° Nose High
30° Nose Low
Weight 1.8g
Weight Zero g
Weight 1.8g
Seconds
0
20
45
65
Did you break anything?
y/n
If yes, what injury did you sustain?
Would you do it again?
y/n

At the same time you could complete these **Things To Do**
08: Realise Your Childhood Dream • 24: See a Space Shuttle Launch • 71: Have Adventurous Sex • 54: Make at Least One Huge Purchase You Can't Afford

See the Aurora Borealis

The Aurora Borealis, or Northern Lights, is a naturally occurring phenomenon caused by charged particles which are ejected from the Sun. When the particles reach Earth, they collide with gas atoms in the Earth's atmosphere causing them to energise, which in turn results in the spectacular multi-coloured light show we see. The focus for the most activity is at the top of the northern hemisphere, due to the effects from the Earth's magnetic field.

Alaska, Canada, Greenland, Iceland, Norway, Russia and Sweden are the best places to see the Northern Lights, the further north the better, although from time to time it is possible to see the Northern Lights further south than usual, due to higher levels of solar activity; but don't wait for the lights to come to you, this only happens once or twice a decade.

Aurora Borealis facts

The best place to see the Aurora Borealis is within the Northern Lights Oval (highlighted by dots)

The Aurora is at its peak during the months of September and March. You can still see the Aurora either side of these months

You may not see the Aurora the first night; be prepared to be there for a few days

The best time of night to see the Aurora is around midnight local time

The Aurora can be seen in the southern hemisphere too

Aurora Borealis in History Cave paintings in southern France depict the Aurora Borealis; the paintings are over 30,000 years old. The oldest writing describing the Aurora Borealis dates back to China in 2,600 B.C.

See the Aurora Borealis **Form**

Once you have completed this **Thing To Do**, stick your Achieved Star here and fill in the form

Achieved

Date and time you saw the Aurora Borealis

d d m m y y y y :

How many days did you have to wait for the lights to appear? Days

Which country were you in when you saw them?

If you didn't see them was this because it was the wrong time of year? y/n

Mark your position on the map with an X

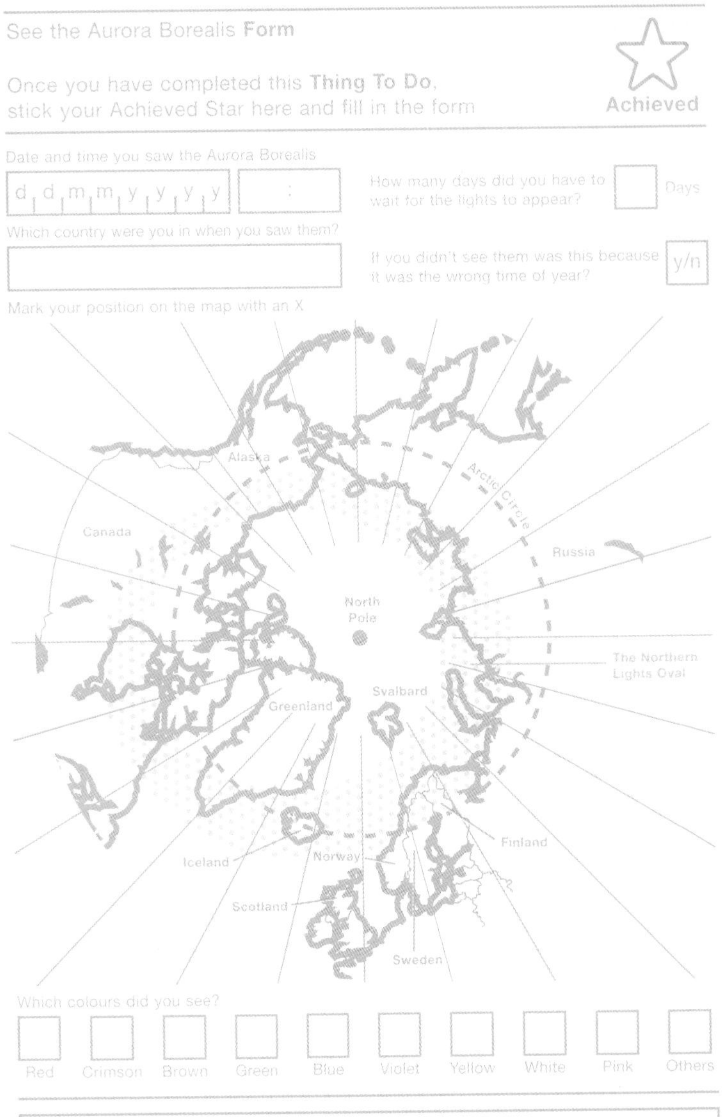

Which colours did you see?

Red | Crimson | Brown | Green | Blue | Violet | Yellow | White | Pink | Others

At the same time you could complete these **Things To Do**
25: Capture the Moment in an Award-winning Photograph • 36: Visit Every Country • 37: Make Fire Without Matches • 71: Have Adventurous Sex

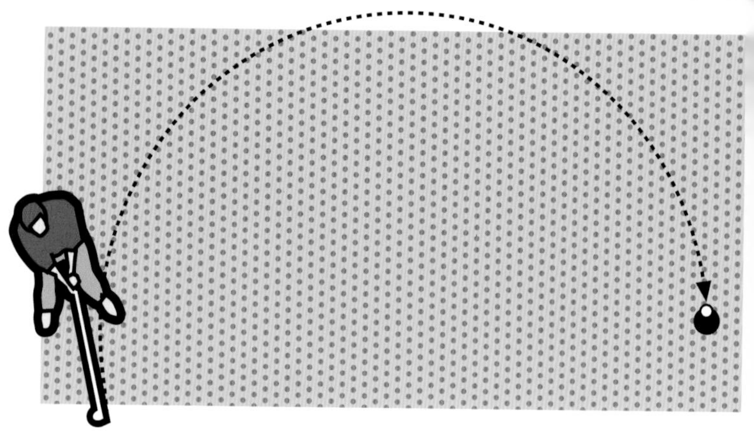

Get to Score a Hole in One

The holy grail of golf, a hole in one. The odds of getting a hole in one for the average golfer is 1 in 42,952. Tiger Woods got his first hole in one at the age of six and it wasn't on the crazy golf course.

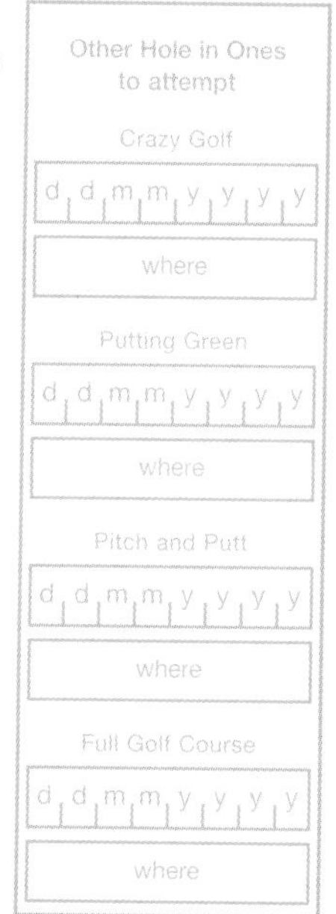

Hole in One Feats

- The longest hole in one was 447 yards, recorded at the Miracle Hills Golf Club in Nebraska by Robert Mitera in 1965
- In 1983 Scott Palmer scored the most holes in one in a single year. He scored 28. All holes were either 3 or 4 par and between 130 yards and 350 yards in length
- It takes an average of 12,000 tee shots to score a hole in one
- The most hole in ones in a career is 68, between 1967 and 1985 by Harry Lee Bonner
- The first recorded hole in one was in 1868 by Tom Morris Jun. at the Prestwick club during the Open Championship

Some Guys Have All the Luck Luck has a lot to do with scoring a hole in one. You could be the best player in the world and go your whole career without scoring a hole in one; on the other hand you could be an amateur and score two hole in ones in a row.

Get to Score a Hole in One **Form**

Once you have completed this **Thing To Do**,
stick your Achieved Star here and fill in the form

Achieved

Date and time

d d m m y y y y :

Which golf course were you on?

Which hole were you on?

What was the par for the hole?

Did you receive a prize for your hole in one?

y/n If yes, what was it?

If it was money how much did you receive?

THINGS TO DO £/$

Did the hole in one occur during a tournament? y/n If yes, which tournament?

What was your overall position in the tournament? Place

How many hole in one witnesses did you have? Name your witnesses below

Witness 1

Witness 2

Length and Height

yds

Approx height you hit the ball

yds

How many years of playing golf did it take before you scored your first hole in one? Yrs

At the same time you could complete these **Things To Do**
03: Win an Award, Trophy or Prize • 16: Get into the *Guinness Book of World Records* • 65: Shout 'Drinks Are on Me!' in a Pub or a Bar

Design Your Own Cocktail

Asking for embarrassingly named cocktails in bars is common practice these days. The cocktails may taste wonderful but the names are designed to make you look stupid. Can you ever look cool asking the barman for an **Orgasm** and two **Urine Samples**? Design your own stupidly named cocktail instead.

Designing Your Cocktail

- Experiment. Throw everything and anything into your cocktail; enjoy the benefits of the taste-testing process
- Learn all the barman skills, including throwing and catching the cocktail shakers and setting fire to fruit juice
- Make sure the cocktail you've devised hasn't already been invented
- Name the cocktail after yourself (see **Thing To Do** No. 94) but if it sounds ridiculous then anything with innuendo will be the perfect substitute

Presentation Use as many accessories as are necessary to make sure your cocktail is memorable. You cannot use too many cocktail umbrellas or hollowed-out pineapples. Use sparklers or go one better and set your cocktail on fire.

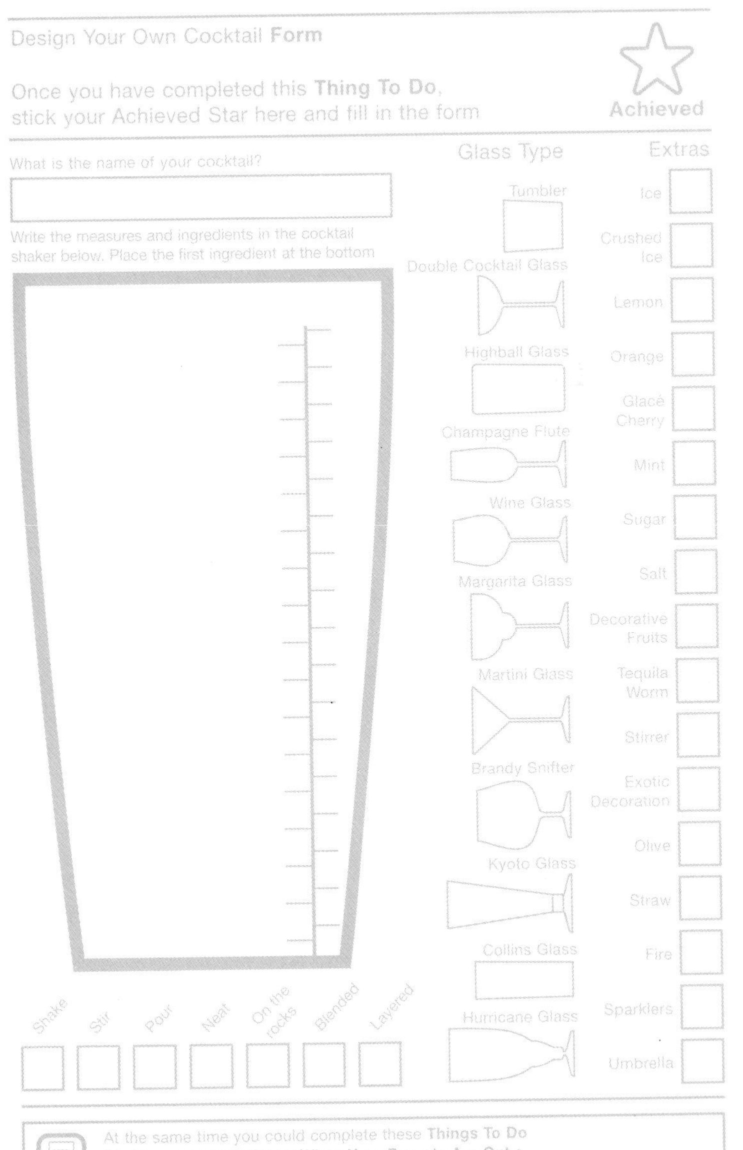
Design Your Own Cocktail **Form**

Once you have completed this **Thing To Do**, stick your Achieved Star here and fill in the form

Achieved

What is the name of your cocktail?

Write the measures and ingredients in the cocktail shaker below. Place the first ingredient at the bottom

Shake
Stir
Pour
Neat
On the rocks
Blended
Layered

Glass Type

Tumbler
Double Cocktail Glass
Highball Glass
Champagne Flute
Wine Glass
Margarita Glass
Martini Glass
Brandy Snifter
Kyoto Glass
Collins Glass
Hurricane Glass

Extras

Ice
Crushed Ice
Lemon
Orange
Glacé Cherry
Mint
Sugar
Salt
Decorative Fruits
Tequila Worm
Stirrer
Exotic Decoration
Olive
Straw
Fire
Sparklers
Umbrella

At the same time you could complete these **Things To Do**
06: Throw a House Party When Your Parents Are Out •
78: Drink a Vintage Wine

Play a Part in Your Favourite TV Show

You've been a loyal follower of the show since it began and you've never missed an episode so it's time you added your name to the cast list.

TV Shows You've Appeared In

TV Shows You've Been in the Audience of

How to Get on Your Favourite Show

- Sign up for extra work. Start off with appearances on adverts and pop videos then move on to hanging around in backgrounds and non-speaking roles. Build up to your debut on your favourite show
- Practise talking without speaking for background work
- Befriend someone who is involved on the show; get them to put in a good word for you
- Write a letter asking to be on the show; if you don't hear back send letter after letter after letter until sheer harassment gets you onto the show
- If you can't get onto the show; at least get into the studio audience and then heckle the warm-up guy

If You Can't Get onto Your Favourite TV Show try and get on a talk show, a quiz show or attempt to be yourself on a reality TV show. If you still have no luck go for the radio phone-in and talk nonsense about anything and everything. Make sure you swear.

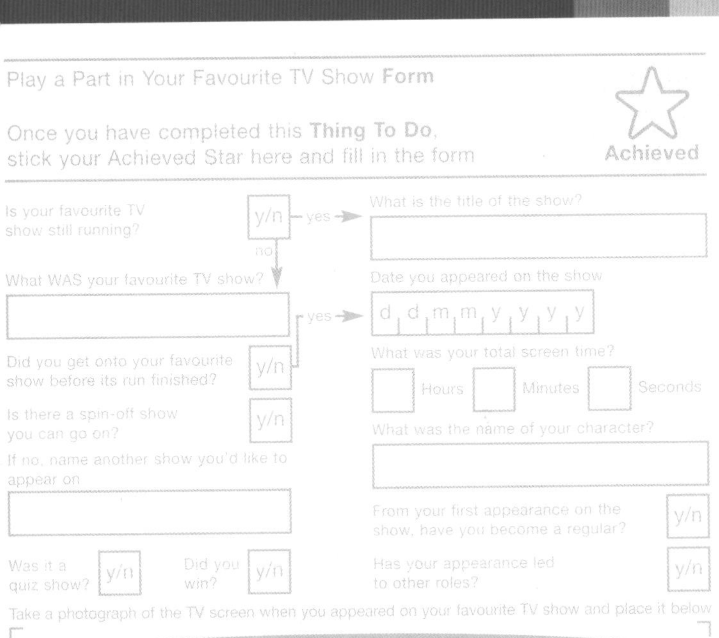

Play a Part in Your Favourite TV Show **Form**

Once you have completed this **Thing To Do**, stick your Achieved Star here and fill in the form

Achieved

Is your favourite TV show still running? y/n — yes → What is the title of the show?

no ↓

What WAS your favourite TV show?

Did you get onto your favourite show before its run finished? y/n — yes → Date you appeared on the show

d d m m y y y y

What was your total screen time?

Hours Minutes Seconds

Is there a spin-off show you can go on? y/n

If no, name another show you'd like to appear on

What was the name of your character?

From your first appearance on the show, have you become a regular? y/n

Was it a quiz show? y/n

Did you win? y/n

Has your appearance led to other roles? y/n

Take a photograph of the TV screen when you appeared on your favourite TV show and place it below

At the same time you could complete these **Things To Do**

29: Meet Your Idol • 30: Stay in the Best Suite in a Five Star Hotel • 63: Make the Front Page of a National Newspaper

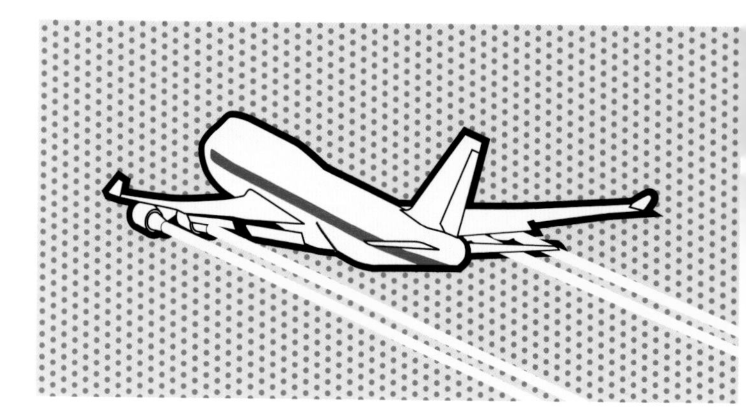

Visit Every Country

Plan A: Visit Every Country

This **Thing To Do** is probably impossible. The only people likely to fill in the achieved star for this **Thing To Do** are politicians, TV holiday show presenters or royalty, and even then these groups will still struggle. Even if you do manage to visit every country, new countries seem to appear every year. The best way to attempt this **Thing To Do** is to visit as many countries as you can, enjoy yourself travelling the world, but mainly, have fun colouring the countries in; after all, there is always Plan B.

Plan B: Visit Every Continent

If visiting every country is too difficult, then you might find it easier to visit each continent instead. Six out of the seven continents are easily accessible, North America, South America, Europe, Africa, Asia, and Australasia. Visiting every continent is definitely the easier option, but don't forget, there's also Antarctica.

Take every opportunity for a holiday. Visit a new country every time. Use those days in lieu you've been saving. **Don't rush**, you've got your whole life to complete this **Thing To Do**. Isn't this what retirement is for?

Visit Every Country **Form**

Once you have completed this **Thing To Do**, stick your Achieved Star here and fill in the form

Achieved

Fill in the country once you've visited it:

At the same time you could complete these **Things To Do**
62: Join the Mile High Club • 43: Throw a Dart into a Map and Travel to Where it Lands • 53: Complete a Coast to Coast Road Trip Across America

Make Fire Without Matches

You'll probably never need to use this survival skill in a real life-or-death situation, but it's a good thing to know just in case.

What You Need

- Find two small stones to strike together
- Gather together items to fuel your fire: moss, lichen, dried grass, and twigs are good for kindling. Use wood for when your fire is established

I'm the Firestarter

- Find a safe place for your fire
- Pile a generous amount of kindling together, take your stones and strike them together next to the kindling to produce sparks; keep trying until the kindling catches
- Once alight, blow on the fire to encourage it to take hold
- Add more kindling and the wood to the growing fire; do not let it go out once lit

How to create fire from the things around you

Flint and steel
strike a penknife or a similar metal object against the flint to produce sparks

A convex lens
Anything with a convex lens, including a camera, a pair of binoculars, a pair of glasses or a magnifying glass. Focus the sun's rays through one of the items mentioned onto the tinder until it smoulders

Batteries
Attach a wire to each terminal of one of the batteries. Hold the battery close to the tinder. Touch the ends of the wires onto the opposite terminals of the other battery together to create sparks

Matches
Dip the heads of matches into candle wax; this way they will be protected from moisture and they'll burn longer and much more fiercely.

Make Fire Without Matches **Form**

Once you have completed this **Thing To Do**, stick your Achieved Star here and fill in the form

Achieved

Fire in the Wilderness

Date you achieved your fire

d d m m y y y y

Where were you?

How did you start the fire?

Stones / Flint and steel / Convex lens / Bow and tinder / Fire drill and bow / Batteries / Lightning / Other

If other, please specify

Was it a life-or-death situation? y/n

If yes, explain what happened

Did the fire save your life? y/n

Did you have to be rescued? y/n

What were the names of your rescuers?

How long did it take you to light the fire?

Straight away / 0–30 minutes / 0–60 minutes / 1–2 hours / 2–4 hours / 4–6 hours / 6–8 hours / Longer

If longer, how long?

Did the fire get out of control? y/n

If yes, explain what happened

How long did it take to put the fire out?

Straight away / Minutes / Hours / Days / Weeks

Did people lose their houses? y/n

Did you get into trouble? y/n

What were the consequences of your actions?

Accidental House Fire

Date you achieved your fire

d d m m y y y y

How did it start?

Faulty Wiring / Gas Leak / Fire not put out properly / Lightning

Explain what happened

At the same time you could complete these **Things To Do**
23: Get Arrested • 60: Take Part in a Police Line-up •
87: Conquer Your Fear • 95: Get Revenge • 99: Confess

See These Animals in the Wild ...

So you've swum with sharks, whales, dolphins and tropical fish (**Thing To Do** No. 2). What next? Come face to face with a gorilla in the rain forests of Africa, ride an elephant in India, chase giraffes on safari and shelter from the cold with emperor penguins in Antarctica.

There are thousands of animals to see in the wild; here are just a few to them for you to hunt down with your high-powered assault camera.

Hunting High and Low

- Make sure you're hunting them and they're not hunting you
- Learn how to stay perfectly still for hours at a time
- Learn to be quiet; leave your mobile phone at home
- Don't get too close or you might not make it back
- Do not feed the animals

Other Animals You've Seen

Animal name here

Animal name here

Animal name here

Animal name here

Animal name here

Animal name here

Animal name here

Animal name here

Animal name here

See all the Animals Native to Your Country Have you ever seen a badger in England, a bald eagle in America or a duck-billed platypus in Australia? Make a list of your country's native animals. Road kill doesn't count.

See These Animals in the Wild ... **Form**

Once you have completed this **Thing To Do**,
stick your Achieved Star here and fill in the form

Achieved

Tick box when you've seen the animal in the wild

Panda
Rhino
Hippo
Grizzly Bear
Elephant
Hummingbird
Giraffe
Koala
Manatee
Gorilla
Lion
Monkey
Penguin
Kangaroo
Tiger
Crocodile
Orangutan
Eagle
Polar Bear
Coelacanth

List the other wild creatures you've seen ...

At the same time you could complete these **Things To Do**
04: Catch a Fish With Your Bare Hands • 22: Go Up in a Hot Air Balloon •
25: Capture the Moment in an Award-winning Photograph • 36: Visit Every Country

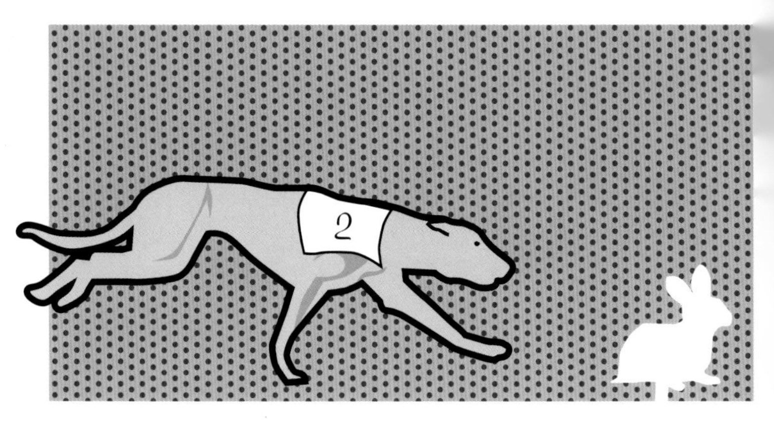

Go to the Dogs

Man's best friend. Humans and dogs have gone hand in paw for centuries. For better and for worse, the human–dog partnership has taken many rocky roads; but, when man and canine work as a team, everyone benefits. The dogs get to run around with their friends and the humans get to sip champagne in the grandstand and make money off the back of their fun. Everyone's a winner!

A Day at the Races

- How old is the greyhound? A dog will peak aged two, a bitch will peak aged three
- Look at its form; how well has it done in the past? Did it run well in its last few races?
- A greyhound's performances can differ from trap to trap. A greyhound that wins from trap 1 may not win when running from trap 4
- Avoid favourites and long shots
- If none of the above works pick dogs with amusing names

Other Forms of Racing

Horse Racing
One of the oldest sports in the world

Ferret Racing and Terrier Racing
Country fair favourites

Camel Racing
Dubai's traditional sport

Bull Racing
The Balinese bull race (Makepung) is held twice a year

Goat Racing
In Trinidad and Tobago jockeys run alongside the goats to make them run as fast as possible

Crab Racing
Also in Trinidad and Tobago, the crabs are jockeyed by sticks. Don't be surprised if the winner gets eaten

Greyhound History Greyhounds have been used as hunting dogs for thousands of years and can be seen in hieroglyphics in the pyramids. The word greyhound comes from Old English *hund*, meaning dog.

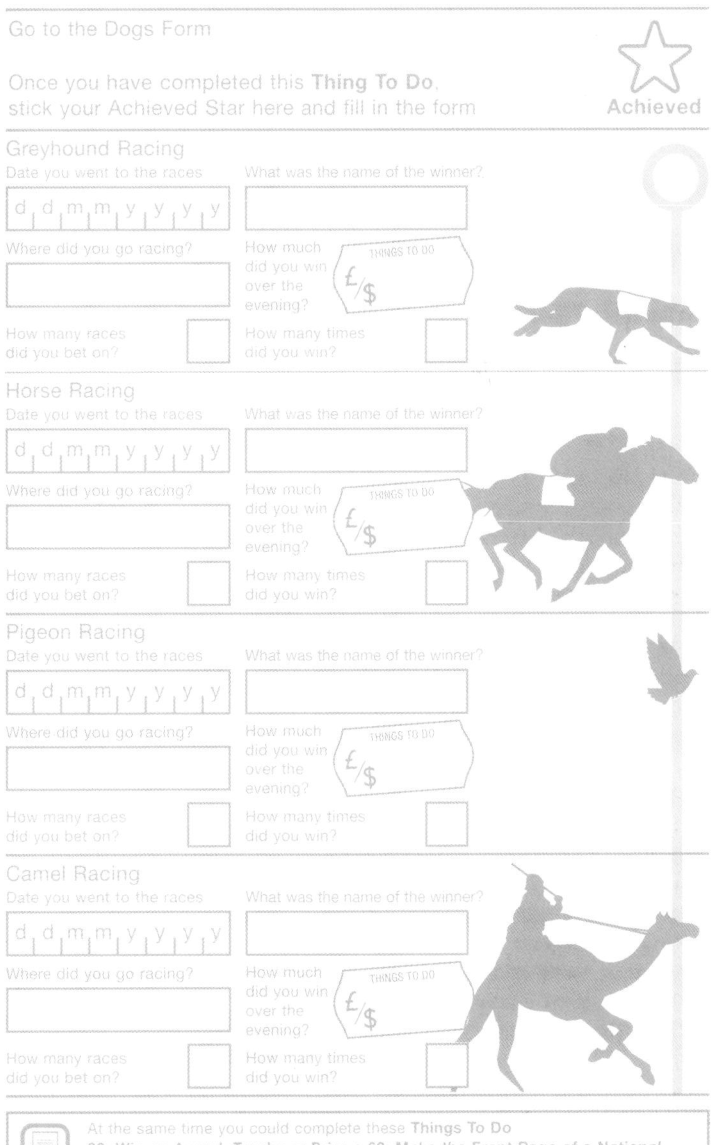

Go to the Dogs Form

Once you have completed this **Thing To Do**, stick your Achieved Star here and fill in the form

Achieved

Greyhound Racing

Date you went to the races: d d m m y y y y

What was the name of the winner?

Where did you go racing?

How much did you win over the evening? THINGS TO DO £/$

How many races did you bet on?

How many times did you win?

Horse Racing

Date you went to the races: d d m m y y y y

What was the name of the winner?

Where did you go racing?

How much did you win over the evening? THINGS TO DO £/$

How many races did you bet on?

How many times did you win?

Pigeon Racing

Date you went to the races: d d m m y y y y

What was the name of the winner?

Where did you go racing?

How much did you win over the evening? THINGS TO DO £/$

How many races did you bet on?

How many times did you win?

Camel Racing

Date you went to the races: d d m m y y y y

What was the name of the winner?

Where did you go racing?

How much did you win over the evening? THINGS TO DO £/$

How many races did you bet on?

How many times did you win?

At the same time you could complete these **Things To Do**
03: Win an Award, Trophy or Prize • 63: Make the Front Page of a National Newspaper • 72: Have Enough Money to Do All the Things on This List

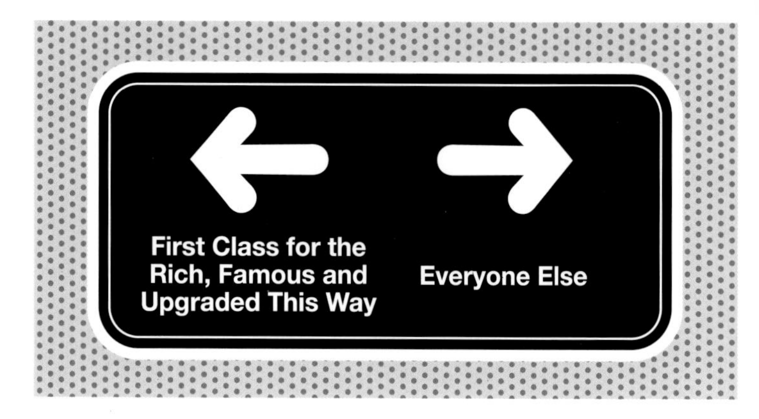

Get a Free Upgrade on a Plane

What goes on behind the blue curtain on a plane? The curtain separates us from them, or rather **them** from **us**. What don't they want us to see? Do they think the peasants will revolt? Are the stewardesses force-feeding the first and business class passengers wine and grapes whilst naked? It's time to get upgraded and find out.

Possible Ways to be Upgraded

- If the flight is over-booked, this makes an upgrade inevitable; make it to the top of their upgrade list
- Dress smartly. If you look like you belong in business class there is a good chance you could get an upgrade
- You can't leap from economy class up to first; economy will be upgraded to the next fare up. You're more likely to get to business class if you have a higher-priced ticket
- It's your birthday/honeymoon/anniversary. Make the staff aware of this fact, but don't lie about your birthday as the real evidence is on your passport
- Put your name on the waiting list for a busy plane; if you get on there's a good chance of an upgrade
- Dress up as a pilot; the airlines look after their own

Special Deals Book the flights for your company's airline trips; this way you'll be the first person the airlines and travel companies will come to with offers and special deals; don't let on about the deals and use them all yourself.

Get a Free Upgrade on a Plane **Form**

Once you have completed this **Thing To Do**, stick your Achieved Star here and fill in the form

Achieved

Date of your upgrade

d d m m y y y y

What type of plane was it?

Which airline were you flying?

Where did you fly from?

and to?

How long was the flight?

Hours Minutes

Mark which class you were supposed to fly and mark the class you were moved up to

Other

Economy Class

Standard Class

Business Class

First Class

Was there a noticeable difference in service? y/n

Who were you with?

If yes, what were the differences?

Did they manage to get an upgrade as well? y/n

Describe how you managed to get an upgrade

At the same time you could complete these **Things To Do**
18: Study the *Kama Sutra* and Put Theory into Practice • 36: Visit Every Country • 62: Join the Mile High Club

Be Friends With Your Ex

Impossible? It doesn't have to be. You were best friends the whole time you were going out until your relationship turned sour. Your friends are her friends, her friends are yours and you get on swimmingly with the parents. Do you really want to lose all that as well as your former love?

Even if you were mismatched (you're an Aquarius, and he/she's a psycho), it's going to be hard but you can work through it, even if the traitor did marry your best friend ...

We Can Work It Out

- Get used to the idea of being apart first. Give each other enough space for the first few months; don't let on about new relationships
- Become Retrosexuals – a retrosexual is a person who has relations with ex-partners more than is common
- But don't go overboard and start demanding he/she take you back; if you think this might occur, put the recovery plan onto the back-burner for another month or two
- Go onto Jerry Springer and talk over your problems in a controlled and open-minded way
- If you can't work it out, find satisfaction by drawing as many pins in the doll which represents them on the form as you think is necessary

Revenge Partnerships
House keys and badly cut new house keys. Scissors and clothes.
Car tyres and sharp knives. Phone booth cards and your ex's phone number.

Be Friends With Your Ex **Form**

Once you have completed this **Thing To Do**, stick your Achieved Star here and fill in the form

Achieved
How long were you together?
Years
Months
Are you still friends?
y/n
If no, why not?
Anything else to add?
Write the name of Ex No.1 here
How long were you together?
Years
Months
Are you still friends?
y/n
If no, why not?
Anything else to add?
Write the name of Ex No.2 here
How long were you together?
Years
Months
Are you still friends?
y/n
If no, why not?
Anything else to add?
Write the name of Ex No.3 here

At the same time you could complete these **Things To Do**

71: Have Adventurous Sex • 95: Get Revenge • 99: Confess

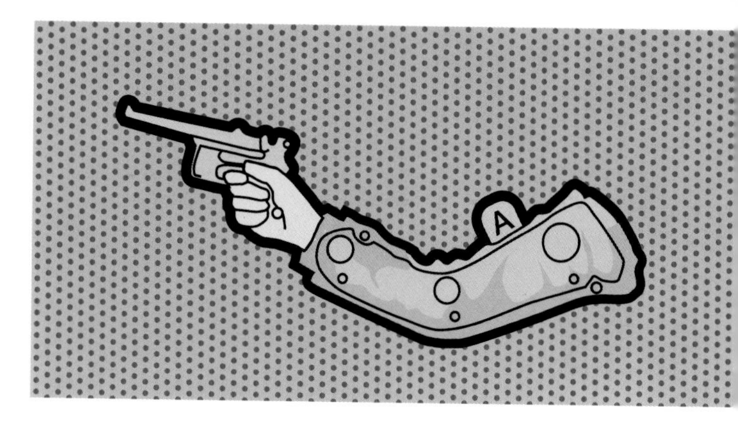

Hit Your Targets

Do you have a stressful job and a slave-driving boss?

Are you under constant pressure to deliver 110% all day, every day?

Are you ready to rip your hair out, scream at the top of your voice ar punch someone?

If this is the case you need some serious time away from the office. Yo could book yourself into a spa for the weekend and be pampered from head to toe. You could escape to the country and the peace and quiet of the wilderness. Or you could relieve your stress on a shooting rang and take all your frustrations out on the cardboard target representing your boss and reap some stress vengeance on your tormentor.

Shoots You, Sir

- Whilst shooting, shout obscenities and hurl abuse. Shout out all the things your boss has wronged you with, 'This one is for __________' and 'This one is for ______________'
- Lob grenades and completely obliterate your target
- Go back to the office on Monday with the knowledge that you dispatched your boss on the weekend
- Don't actually dispatch your boss

Stress Management In some offices in Japan, you can take your frustrations out on your boss by beating him up. In the basement, straw effigies are constructed, which feature masks of the company hierarchy. You can attack them with a Japanese Jo fighting stick.

Hit Your Targets **Form**

Once you have completed this **Thing To Do**, stick your Achieved Star here and fill in the form

At the same time you could complete these **Things To Do**

03: Win an Award, Trophy or Prize • 59: Leave a Job You Hate • 99: Confess

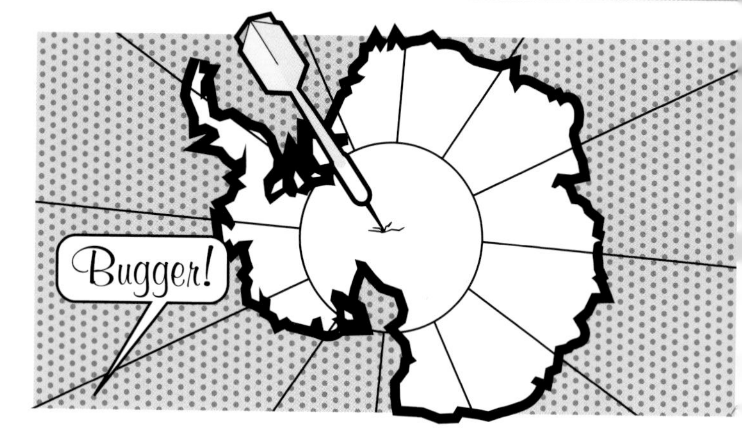

Throw a Dart into a Map and Travel to Where it Lands

Stuck for a place to take your next holiday? Or just bored and need something to do? This is the **Thing To Do** for you.

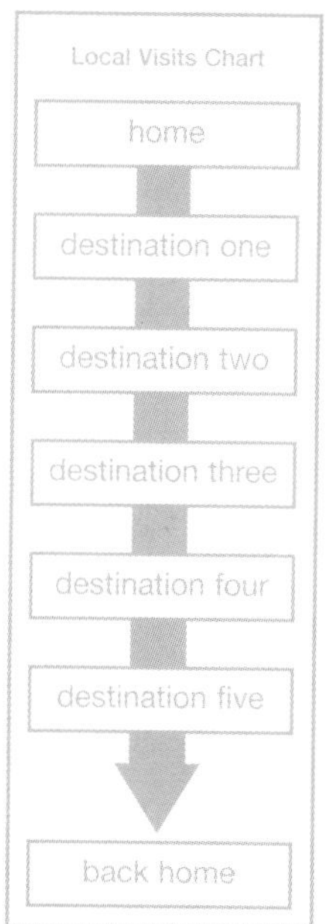

Global Visits

Items Needed: A Dart, Blindfold, World Map

Blindfolded, throw the dart into the world map, take the blindfold off and see where the dart has landed. Visit the country the dart landed on. When you are there visit the exact place where the dart landed.

Local Visits

Items Needed: A Dart, Blindfold, Local Map, Car

Nothing to do this weekend? Find a local map, approximately 60 square miles around your home. Blindfolded, throw your dart into the map; travel to your destination. After a look around, repeat this process five times before heading home.

Rules

If your dart lands in the sea, throw again (unless you own a yacht).
Collect fridge magnets as proof of your visits. Never visit the same place twice.

Throw a Dart into a Map and Travel to Where it Lands **Form**

Once you have completed this **Thing To Do**, stick your Achieved Star here and fill in the form

Achieved

Date and time of dart-throwing

d d m m y y y y :

What area is the map of?

What is the name of the exact place the dart landed?

Which country, county or state did the dart land in?

Have you been there before? y/n

If yes, when?

d d m m y y y y

Did you cheat? y/n

How did you cheat?

Date and time of your trip

d d m m y y y y :

How long did you stay?

How did you get there?

Did you visit the exact place where the dart landed? y/n

If yes, what did you find there?

Who were you with?

If no, why didn't you visit the exact spot?

At the same time you could complete these **Things To Do**
36: Visit Every Country • 42: Hit Your Targets • 67: Visit ... • 71: Have Adventurous Sex • 97: Live Out of a Van

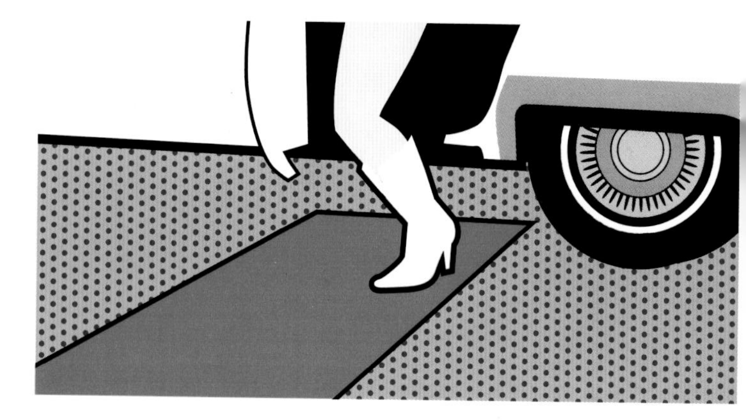

Attend a Film Premiere

Put on your fancy frock and join in with the celebrity enjoyed by Hollywood's Glitterazzi. Hire a limousine and arrive in style. Walk the full length of the red carpet, wave at the thousands of fans behind the barriers and see if they wave back at you. Go over to them, sign autographs and pose for photos.

Rub shoulders with the rich, famous and royal. Stand next to Tom Cruise and compare heights, challenge Russell Crowe to a drinking competition and see how real you look compared to Meg Ryan.

After the movie, try to gatecrash the aftershow party (see **Thing To Do** No. 56). If you do get in, get photographed with as many celebrities as you can. If you get thrown out shout, 'Do you know who I am?' and 'I can get you fired!' at the top of your voice, take down the bouncer's name and tell him that you are 'going to have his legs broken'.

If you don't actually manage to do any of the above, at least make sure you go home with a souvenir programme and goody bag; at least you can make some money on eBay as a consolation.

Ticket and Programme Sell the freebies you get on eBay (try to get the stars of the film to sign the programme first). Sell the items before the film goes on general release: if the film is rubbish, they'll be worth more before the film than after.

Attend a Film Premiere **Form**

Once you have completed this **Thing To Do**, stick your Achieved Star here and fill in the form

Achieved

Date and time of premiere

d d m m y y y y :

Which film was the premiere for?

Where was the premiere?

How did you get your ticket?

Did you walk the full length of the red carpet? y/n

Did you get your photo taken by the paparazzi? y/n

If yes, did you see a photo of yourself at the premiere in a paper or magazine? y/n

Which famous people were at the premiere?

Did you meet any of them?

y/n If yes, who?

Did you sit next to anyone famous?

y/n If yes, who?

Did you get a souvenir programme?

y/n If yes, did you sell it on eBay and make money from it? y/n

The Film

How would you rate the film?

Poor OK Good Very Good Excellent

Did it live up to the hype? y/n

If no, write your reasons why not below

Did you go to the aftershow party? y/n

If yes, which famous guests did you see?

Autograph area

At the same time you could complete these **Things To Do**

29: Meet Your Idol • 57: See the All-time Greatest Films • 84: Sell All Your Junk on eBay and Make a Profit • 96: Be an Extra in a Film

Do a Runner From a Fancy Restaurant

Whatever your reason for skipping out without paying from a restaurant, whether it's because the food is terrible, the surly waiters, the price or just for the hell of it – make sure you've done your homework first. Try not to pick a venue with a maître d' at the front of the restaurant, that's just asking to get caught. Pick a restaurant that can afford to soak up your hefty bill. Don't pick a small business, you don't want to bankrupt them.

Born to Run

- Sit as near to the door as possible; if this isn't possible, plan the shortest route to the exit, be cool and confident as you stroll out
- Order the more expensive items that you wouldn't normally have due to the inflated prices, but don't go for the hugely expensive items such as champagne. Try to keep a low profile
- Don't put your coat in the cloakroom. Once you're out the door there's no going back
- Don't give out your credit card details before the meal when booking your table; if you do a runner, the restaurant can get their revenge by adding more to your bill as you haven't got a receipt to prove otherwise

Foot the Bill If you are with a big group and you've decided to do a runner, under no circumstances should you go to the toilet towards the end of the meal. If the rest of your group do a runner while you're indisposed, you'll end up well and truly inconvenienced.

Do a Runner From a Fancy Restaurant **Form**

Once you have completed this **Thing To Do**, stick your Achieved Star here and fill in the form

Achieved

Date and time you did a runner

d d m m y y y y :

Which restaurant were you dining in?

Was it a conscious decision? y/n

Or did you accidentally forget to pay? y/n

Was there a maitre d' to escape past? y/n

What did you eat and drink?

What was the most expensive item you ordered?

How did you escape?

Front door

Through the toilet window

Through the kitchens

Emergency exit

Do you know how much the bill was for? Place the total below. If you ran before the bill arrived, estimate the total

THANK YOU

FOR YOUR CUSTOM

PLEASE CALL AGAIN

How many people were dining?

How many separate items did you have?

How many drinks did you have?

Do you know if someone else had to foot the bill? y/n

OVERALL TOTAL

Did you get caught? y/n

If yes, what were the consequences?

Have you been back since? y/n

At the same time you could complete these **Things To Do**

23: Get Arrested • 78: Drink a Vintage Wine • 95: Get Revenge

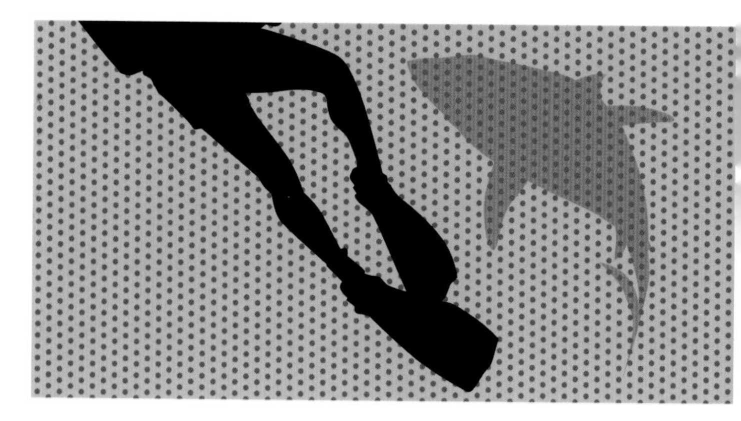

Scuba Dive

Scuba diving or **S**elf-**C**ontained **U**nderwater **B**reathing **A**pparatus Diving, to give it its full name, is enjoyed by thousands of people on vacation every year, trying to get glimpses of tropical fish, coral, shipwrecks, turtles, sharks and other underwater living things. Before you scuba dive you've got to be 100% sure you want to because once you're under the water nobody can hear you scream. If you don't think you can do it, stick to snorkelling.

Under Pressure

- If you're scared of fish, don't dive
- You should be a good swimmer; you could be in the water for hours at a time
- Never swim alone. If you get into trouble who is going to help you?
- You don't need a diving certificate if you are scuba diving on holiday but if you want to do it again, get qualified, then you can use your diver's card all over the world
- Leave the wildlife alone. Don't attempt to steal the coral, it will cut your hands to shreds and the blood gushing from your hand will attract sharks and you'll get eaten alive

The Deepest Scuba Dive stands at 1,026.9ft, (313m) by Mark Ellyatt, a British diving instructor in Thailand. On 4 January 2004 it took 12 minutes to descend to this depth but it took 6 hours and 40 minutes to return to the surface, for safety reasons.

Scuba Dive **Form**

Once you have completed this **Thing To Do**, stick your Achieved Star here and fill in the form

Mark on the diagram the greatest depth you've swum down to. Draw the creatures on the diagram at the depth you saw them

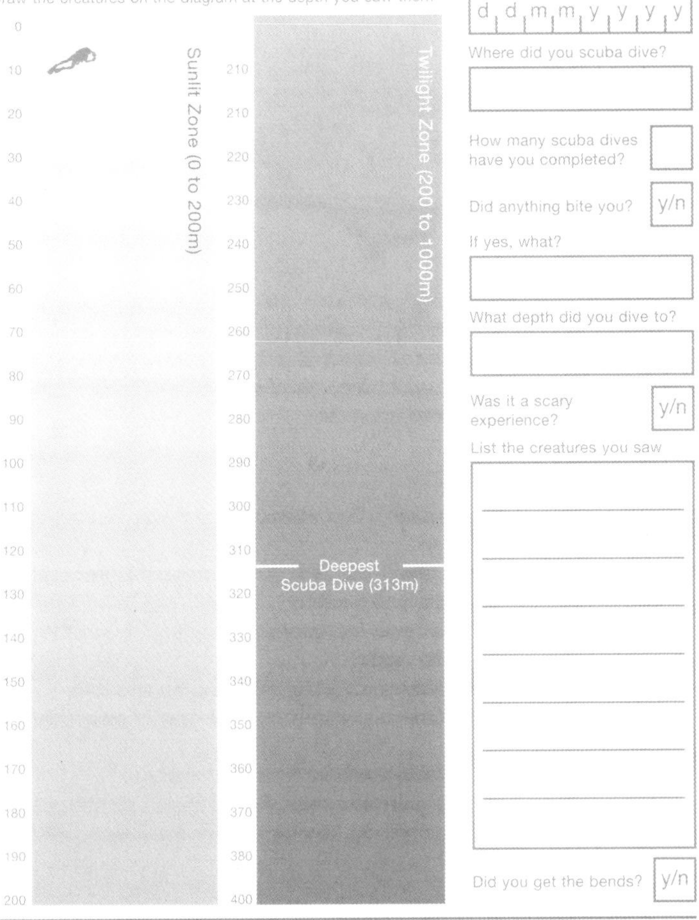

Date you scuba dived

d d m m y y y y

Where did you scuba dive?

How many scuba dives have you completed?

Did anything bite you? y/n

If yes, what?

What depth did you dive to?

Was it a scary experience? y/n

List the creatures you saw

Did you get the bends? y/n

At the same time you could complete these **Things To Do**
02: Swim With ... 05: Make a Discovery • 16: Get into the *Guinness Book of World Records* • 38: See These Animals in the Wild ...

Milk a Cow

The average cow produces 7 gallons of milk a day, which is equivalent to 90 glasses of milk. Everything these days is automated, pre-packaged and shrink-wrapped. It seems nothing is done manually anymore; time to get back to basics. All you have to do is get that milk out of the cow and into your tea.

How to Milk a Cow

- Milk the cow before or after it has eaten. Do not milk a cow while it is eating
- Make sure the udder is clean, you don't want manure in your milk
- Place a bucket under your cow's udder
- Start with one teat. Once you feel confident and you've got the hang of milking, use both hands
- Use each hand on separate teats. Using your thumb and fore-finger, pinch the teat at the top, then close the rest of your fingers around the teat
- Release your pinch and allow milk to flow into the teat
- With firm pressure with your last three fingers draw out the milk
- Work both hands into a rhythm, keeping a constant flow of milk

Dairy cows provide 90% of the world's milk
If you haven't got a cow to hand, you could try other beasts which can also be milked, such as goats, sheep, camels, reindeer, buffalo and even horses.

Milk a Cow **Form**

Once you have completed this **Thing To Do**, stick your Achieved Star here and fill in the form

Achieved

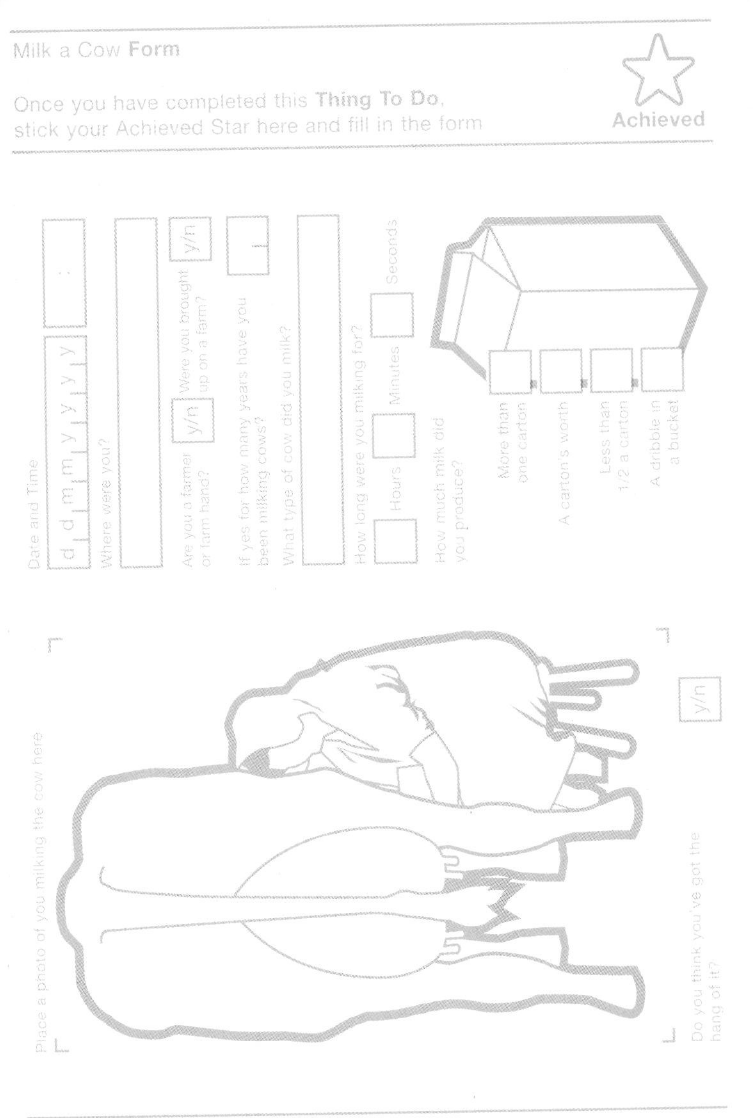

Date and Time
d d m m y y y y
:
Where were you?
Are you a farmer or farm hand?
y/n
Were you brought up on a farm?
y/n
If yes for how many years have you been milking cows?
What type of cow did you milk?
How long were you milking for?
Hours
Minutes
Seconds
How much milk did you produce?
More than one carton
A carton's worth
Less than 1/2 a carton
A dribble in a bucket
Place a photo of you milking the cow here
Do you think you've got the hang of it?
y/n

At the same time you could complete these **Things To Do**

34: Design Your Own Cocktail • 66: Be Part of a Flash Mob

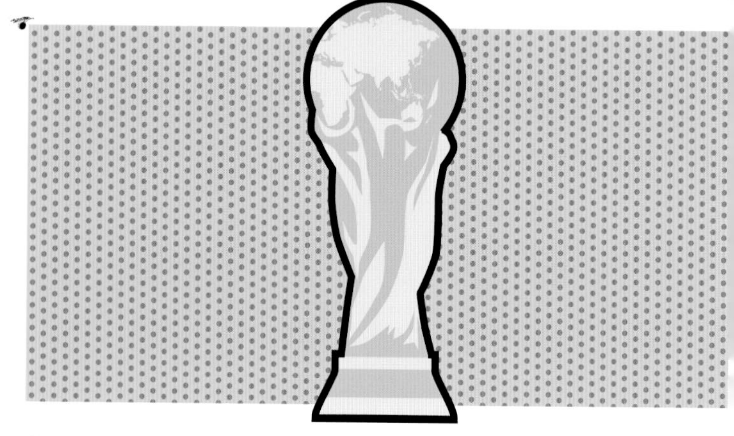

Be Present When Your Country Wins the World Cup

Every four years a worldwide sporting phenomenon occurs. People get ready for a four week emotional rollercoaster ride of goals, near misses, sendings-off and penalties. No other tournament in the world can compare to the excitement generated by the football World Cup. In 2002, it is estimated that a worldwide TV audience of 1.3 billion people watched the final between Brazil and Germany.

Prepare for the World Cup

- Be organised well in advance; the demand for tickets is enormous; the sooner you become part of the supporters' club the better
- Buy your tickets before you arrive at the venue. Ticket touts will charge you ten times more than you would have originally paid
- If you can't get a ticket try posing as a member of the press and walk in. If all else fails, beg steal or borrow to get to the final

Football World Cup Winners

- Year **Winner** (Host) -

1930 **Uruguay** (Uruguay)
1934 **Italy** (Italy)
1938 **Italy** (France)
1950 **Uruguay** (Brazil)
1954 **W. Germany** (Switzerland)
1958 **Brazil** (Sweden)
1962 **Brazil** (Chile)
1966 **England** (England)
1970 **Brazil** (Mexico)
1974 **W. Germany** (Germany)
1978 **Argentina** (Argentina)
1982 **Italy** (Spain)
1986 **Argentina** (Mexico)
1990 **W. Germany** (Italy)
1994 **Brazil** (USA)
1998 **France** (France)
2002 **Brazil** (Korea/Japan)

Rugby World Cup Winners

1987 **New Zealand** (Australia & New Zealand)
1991 **Australia** (UK, Ireland & France)
1995 **South Africa** (South Africa)
1999 **Australia** (Wales)
2003 **England** (Australia)

World Team Competitions
The Fifa world cup is the biggest team event in the world (the Olympics is the biggest sports event in the world, but not a single team event); the rugby world cup is second.

Be Present When Your Country Wins the World Cup **Form**

Once you have completed this **Thing To Do**, stick your Achieved Star here and fill in the form

Achieved

Date of final

d d m m y y y y

Which teams were in the final?

v

Did the match go to penalties?

What time was the kick-off? :

What was the full-time score? :

What was the final score? :

Who scored and in which minute(s)?

How much did your ticket cost? THINGS TO DO £/$

Was it worth every penny? y/n

Place an 'X' approximately where you were sitting on the seating plan below

Which country hosted the World Cup finals?

What was the name of the stadium the final was played in?

What was the capacity of the stadium (in thousands)?

At the same time you could complete these **Things To Do**

55: Score the Winning Goal / Try / Basket • 65: Shout 'Drinks Are on Me!' in a Pub or a Bar • 69: In Various Languages, Learn to Say ...

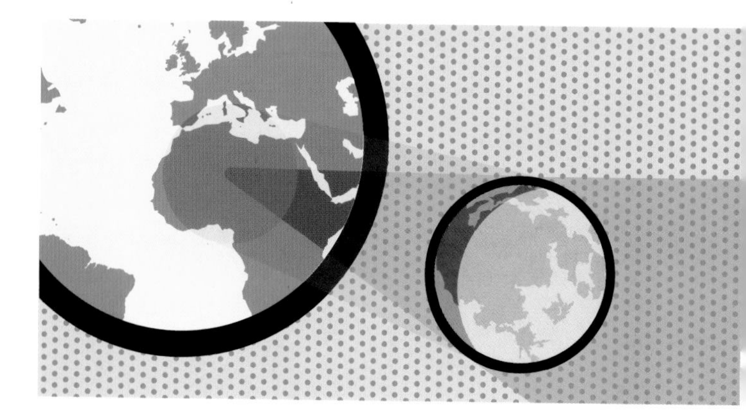

See Both Solar and Lunar Eclipses

For the first time in 72 years, a total eclipse was to hit England. On 11 August 1999, the people of Cornwall gathered (the only part of Britain to see a total eclipse). TV crews arrived to broadcast the event live as this was to be the last eclipse in England in our lifetime (the next one is due in 2090). As thousands of people gathered to see the eclipse at its totality, so did the clouds. The spectacular event happened, but the people of Cornwall didn't get to see it, they got to see something a little more familiar, a blanket of cloud. It turns out the people who stayed in their homes got a far better view of the total eclipse.

Dos and Don'ts

- **Don't** look directly into the sun with your naked eye. If you do, your lens will act like a magnifying glass and burn a hole into the back of your eye
- **Do** choose a country with good weather

Types of Eclipse

Total
Solar When the sun is covered by the moon
Lunar When the Earth travels between the sun and the moon

Partial
Solar When part of the moon's shadow touches the Earth
Lunar When part of the Earth's shadow touches the moon

Annular
Solar When the moon is in front of the sun but it appears smaller

Hybrid
Solar When one kind of eclipse is seen in one part of the world and a total eclipse is seen in another at the same time

Penumbral
Lunar When the Earth's penumbra, the lighter part of the Earth's shadow, travels across the moon

What Happens During a Total Eclipse As the moon crosses the path of the sun the temperature starts to drop, day turns into night as it gets darker and the birds stop singing as they think its dusk. The stars appear at the point of totality.

See both Solar and Lunar Eclipses **Form**

Once you have completed this **Thing To Do**, stick your Achieved Star here and fill in the form

Achieved

Date of the **Solar** Eclipse

d d m m y y y y

Where did you see the eclipse?

What was the weather like?

Did the weather spoil your view? y/n If yes, how much did you see in % %

Draw what you saw

Sun

Time at the height of the eclipse : AM PM

What type of eclipse was it?

- **Total**
- **Partial**
- **Annular**
- **Hybrid**

The next 5 **Total Solar Eclipses** ...

- 29.03.06 Central Africa, Turkey & Russia
- 01.08.06 N. Canada, China, Mongolia, Siberia & Greenland
- 22.07.09 India, Nepal, Central Pacific & China
- 11.07.10 South Pacific, Easter Island, Chile & Argentina
- 13.11.12 North Australia & South Pacific

Date of the **Lunar** Eclipse

d d m m y y y y

Where did you see the eclipse?

What was the weather like?

Did the weather spoil your view? y/n If yes, how much did you see in % %

Draw what you saw

Time at the height of the eclipse : AM PM

What type of eclipse was it?

- **Total**
- **Partial**
- **Penumbral**

The next 5 **Total Lunar Eclipses** ...

- 28.10.04 Americas, Europe, Africa & Central Asia
- 03.03.07 Americas, Europe, Africa & Asia
- 28.08.07 East Asia, Australia, Pacific & Americas
- 21.02.08 Central Pacific, Americas, Europe & Africa
- 21.12.10 East Asia, Australia, Pacific, Americas & Europe

At the same time you could complete these **Things To Do**
25: Capture the Moment in an Award-winning Photograph • 63: Make the Front Page of a National Newspaper

Write Your Name Over a Star on the Walk of Fame

There are over 2,000 stars on Hollywood Boulevard, featuring some of the most notable names in stage and screen. It began in 1960 and in recent times approximately two stars per month are added. The five star categories include contribution to film, television, radio, the recording industry and live theatre. There are hundreds of famous names; some are are a little more obscure, but there's no doubt that if anyone deserved a star it's **Big Bird**.

What You Need

- A stick of chalk and a camera

What To Do

- Choose the star of someone who you think doesn't deserve to be there, chalk your name over the top of theirs and take a photo as evidence. Leave your name scrawled on the floor and walk away
- Walk up to Mann's Chinese Theatre and get lost in the crowd; while you're there check out Darth Vader's footprints and Groucho Marx's cigar. Take in a movie and by the time the film finishes any trouble your actions have caused will have dissipated. Go back to the star and see if your name is still there

Mann's Chinese Theatre (formally Grauman's Chinese Theater) The first hand prints to be laid were by Mary Pickford and Douglas Fairbanks in 1927. At present there are 173 prints, including prints of famous robots, horses, guns, limbs and noses.

Write Your Name Over a Star on the Walk of Fame **Form**

Once you have completed this **Thing To Do**, stick your Achieved Star here and fill in the form

Date and time

d d m m y y y y | :

Write in the name of the person who the star was attributed to, then recreate your name scrawled over it; draw in the symbol of their profession in the circle. Alternatively place a photograph here

Did you chose someone who you really dislike?

y/n If no, why did you pick this person?

Were there any consequences of your actions?

y/n If yes, what were they?

At the same time you could complete these **Things To Do**

23: Get Arrested • 10: Leave Your Mark in Graffiti • 29: Meet Your Idol

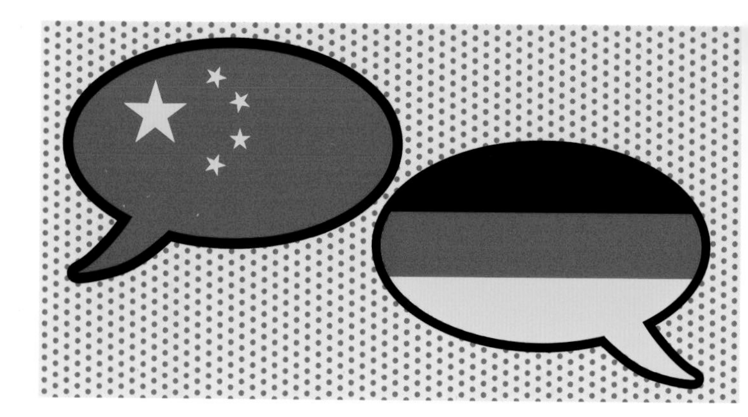

Learn Another Language

Everyone knows there are more opportunities for those people who can speak more than one language. Bilingual children have a head start on the rest of us. Scientific studies show that it is easier to learn new languages and other new skills if exposed to more than one language at an early age.

So where does that leave the rest of us? It leaves us with gaping hole on our Curriculum Vitae advertising the fact we are linguistically inept. We could put "French" from the tiny bit that we learned at school, but asking 'Where is the Police Station?' and 'Have you got anything cheaper?' will only get you so far in the fast-moving world of international commerce.

It's high time you did something about it. Buy yourself a language-learning CD or tape from the back of a newspaper; you can learn a new language while you're driving around in your car. Be prepared for the strange looks you'll get from passers-by as you loudly repeat 'My house is on fire, please call the emergency services' in Japanese.

World Languages
There are approximately 6,700 languages in the world, spoken in 228 countries. Mandarin is the most widely spoken first language in the world.

Learn Another Language **Form**

Once you have completed this **Thing To Do**,
stick your Achieved Star here and fill in the form

Achieved

Write in the languages you speak below. Write your first language in the first bubble

I can speak

Write language in here

Badly / OK / Well / Fluently*

I can also speak

Write language in here

Badly / OK / Well / Fluently*

and

Write language in here

Badly / OK / Well / Fluently*

... I can also speak [ ] other languages than the three mentioned

* Delete where applicable

At the same time you could complete these **Things To Do**

36: Visit Every Country • 69: In Various Languages, Learn to Say ...

Read the Greatest Books Ever Written

Reading the most celebrated books is one of those things you never get around to doing. You know they're going to be around for ever and they're not likely to go out of print soon, so what's the hurry?

There are plenty of lists on the internet on which to base your greatest books. Depending on which list you look at, some say *The Adventures of Huckleberry Finn* by Mark Twain is the greatest book, others say *1984* by George Orwell and the classic book lists contain Chaucer, Kafka, Dostoevsky, Shakespeare and Dickens among others.

Find the kind of books you like reading and use these as a basis for your list, as *War and Peace* by Tolstoy isn't everyone's cup of tea. Don't wait until the movie comes out, pick up a book and use your imagination instead. Here is a list of books to get you started. Some of the books appear on the greatest books of all time list, others wouldn't make the list even if they were the only books left in existence ...

How to Get Everyone Reading

- Start a book group
- Start a 'community read-in', a new phenomenon which entails people in the same region reading the same book at the same time
- Leave your favourite book on a bus for someone else to read

The Greatest Book of the Twentieth Century
The Lord of the Rings by J.R.R. Tolkien. It has been translated into 25 languages and has sold over 100 million copies worldwide.

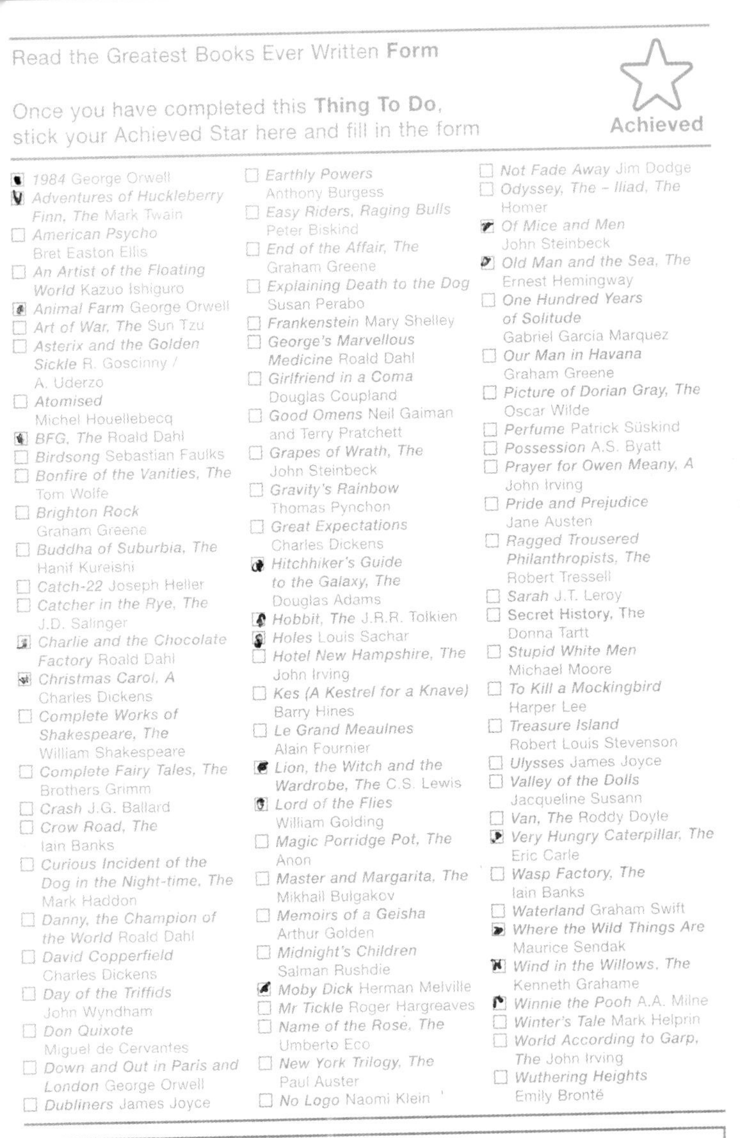

Read the Greatest Books Ever Written **Form**

Once you have completed this **Thing To Do**, stick your Achieved Star here and fill in the form

Achieved

- [x] *1984* George Orwell
- [x] *Adventures of Huckleberry Finn, The* Mark Twain
- [ ] *American Psycho* Bret Easton Ellis
- [ ] *An Artist of the Floating World* Kazuo Ishiguro
- [x] *Animal Farm* George Orwell
- [ ] *Art of War, The* Sun Tzu
- [ ] *Asterix and the Golden Sickle* R. Goscinny / A. Uderzo
- [ ] *Atomised* Michel Houellebecq
- [x] *BFG, The* Roald Dahl
- [ ] *Birdsong* Sebastian Faulks
- [ ] *Bonfire of the Vanities, The* Tom Wolfe
- [ ] *Brighton Rock* Graham Greene
- [ ] *Buddha of Suburbia, The* Hanif Kureishi
- [ ] *Catch-22* Joseph Heller
- [ ] *Catcher in the Rye, The* J.D. Salinger
- [x] *Charlie and the Chocolate Factory* Roald Dahl
- [x] *Christmas Carol, A* Charles Dickens
- [ ] *Complete Works of Shakespeare, The* William Shakespeare
- [ ] *Complete Fairy Tales, The* Brothers Grimm
- [ ] *Crash* J.G. Ballard
- [ ] *Crow Road, The* Iain Banks
- [ ] *Curious Incident of the Dog in the Night-time, The* Mark Haddon
- [ ] *Danny, the Champion of the World* Roald Dahl
- [ ] *David Copperfield* Charles Dickens
- [ ] *Day of the Triffids* John Wyndham
- [ ] *Don Quixote* Miguel de Cervantes
- [ ] *Down and Out in Paris and London* George Orwell
- [ ] *Dubliners* James Joyce
- [ ] *Earthly Powers* Anthony Burgess
- [ ] *Easy Riders, Raging Bulls* Peter Biskind
- [ ] *End of the Affair, The* Graham Greene
- [ ] *Explaining Death to the Dog* Susan Perabo
- [ ] *Frankenstein* Mary Shelley
- [ ] *George's Marvellous Medicine* Roald Dahl
- [ ] *Girlfriend in a Coma* Douglas Coupland
- [ ] *Good Omens* Neil Gaiman and Terry Pratchett
- [ ] *Grapes of Wrath, The* John Steinbeck
- [ ] *Gravity's Rainbow* Thomas Pynchon
- [ ] *Great Expectations* Charles Dickens
- [x] *Hitchhiker's Guide to the Galaxy, The* Douglas Adams
- [x] *Hobbit, The* J.R.R. Tolkien
- [x] *Holes* Louis Sachar
- [ ] *Hotel New Hampshire, The* John Irving
- [ ] *Kes (A Kestrel for a Knave)* Barry Hines
- [ ] *Le Grand Meaulnes* Alain Fournier
- [x] *Lion, the Witch and the Wardrobe, The* C.S. Lewis
- [x] *Lord of the Flies* William Golding
- [ ] *Magic Porridge Pot, The* Anon
- [ ] *Master and Margarita, The* Mikhail Bulgakov
- [ ] *Memoirs of a Geisha* Arthur Golden
- [ ] *Midnight's Children* Salman Rushdie
- [x] *Moby Dick* Herman Melville
- [ ] *Mr Tickle* Roger Hargreaves
- [ ] *Name of the Rose, The* Umberto Eco
- [ ] *New York Trilogy, The* Paul Auster
- [ ] *No Logo* Naomi Klein
- [ ] *Not Fade Away* Jim Dodge
- [ ] *Odyssey, The – Iliad, The* Homer
- [x] *Of Mice and Men* John Steinbeck
- [x] *Old Man and the Sea, The* Ernest Hemingway
- [ ] *One Hundred Years of Solitude* Gabriel Garcia Marquez
- [ ] *Our Man in Havana* Graham Greene
- [ ] *Picture of Dorian Gray, The* Oscar Wilde
- [ ] *Perfume* Patrick Süskind
- [ ] *Possession* A.S. Byatt
- [ ] *Prayer for Owen Meany, A* John Irving
- [ ] *Pride and Prejudice* Jane Austen
- [ ] *Ragged Trousered Philanthropists, The* Robert Tressell
- [ ] *Sarah* J.T. Leroy
- [ ] Secret History, The Donna Tartt
- [ ] *Stupid White Men* Michael Moore
- [ ] *To Kill a Mockingbird* Harper Lee
- [ ] *Treasure Island* Robert Louis Stevenson
- [ ] *Ulysses* James Joyce
- [ ] *Valley of the Dolls* Jacqueline Susann
- [ ] *Van, The* Roddy Doyle
- [x] *Very Hungry Caterpillar, The* Eric Carle
- [ ] *Wasp Factory, The* Iain Banks
- [ ] *Waterland* Graham Swift
- [x] *Where the Wild Things Are* Maurice Sendak
- [x] *Wind in the Willows, The* Kenneth Grahame
- [x] *Winnie the Pooh* A.A. Milne
- [ ] *Winter's Tale* Mark Helprin
- [ ] *World According to Garp, The* John Irving
- [ ] *Wuthering Heights* Emily Brontë

At the same time you could complete these **Things To Do**

01: Write a Best-seller

Complete a Coast to Coast Road Trip Across America

You've seen the trip in movies, so why not do the journey yourself? Start your 3,000-mile journey in New York* and end it in San Francisco*, taking in the sights of middle America along the way. Gather a handful of friends together (preferably ones that can drive), live out of a camper van for a few weeks (see **Thing To Do** No. 97), and hit the open road.

Before you start your adventure, revise with *Easy Rider*, *Vanishing Point*, *Thelma and Louise* and *The Straight Story*. Avoid situations such as sharing your journey with lunatics (*Kalifornia*), staying in a motel where the owner is a *Psycho* or the deranged try to kill you with power tools (*The Texas Chainsaw Massacre*). If you see anything suspicious get out of your van and investigate. What's the worst that could happen?

* Your destinations may vary

Towns, Cities and Sights Visited

Route 66 Originally ran from Chicago to Santa Monica, although it doesn't exist anymore. Only a small portion of Route 66 remains as a highway between San Dimas and San Bernardino, although it is now known as SR 66.

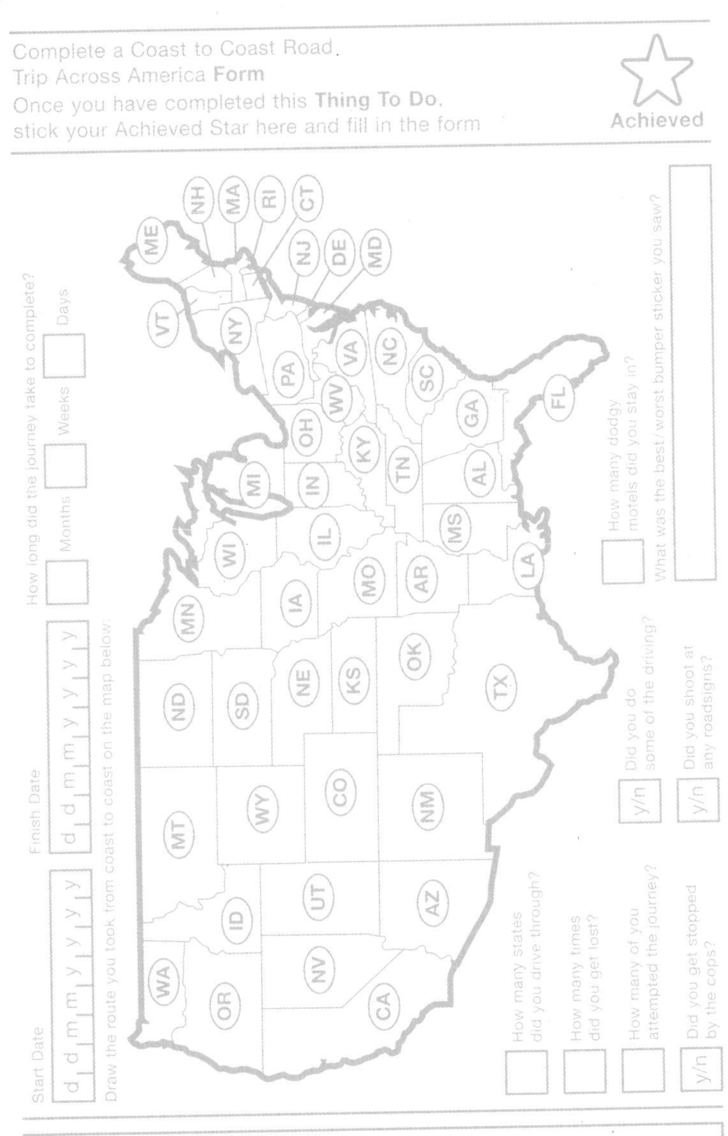

Complete a Coast to Coast Road Trip Across America **Form**

Once you have completed this **Thing To Do**, stick your Achieved Star here and fill in the form

Achieved

Start Date d d m m y y y y

Finish Date d d m m y y y y

How long did the journey take to complete? Months Weeks Days

Draw the route you took from coast to coast on the map below:

How many states did you drive through?

How many times did you get lost?

How many of you attempted the journey?

Did you get stopped by the cops? y/n

Did you do some of the driving? y/n

Did you shoot at any roadsigns? y/n

How many dodgy motels did you stay in?

What was the best/worst bumper sticker you saw?

At the same time you could complete these **Things To Do**
43: Throw a Dart into a Map and Travel to Where it Lands • 50: Write Your Name Over a Star on the Walk of Fame • 97: Live Out of a Van

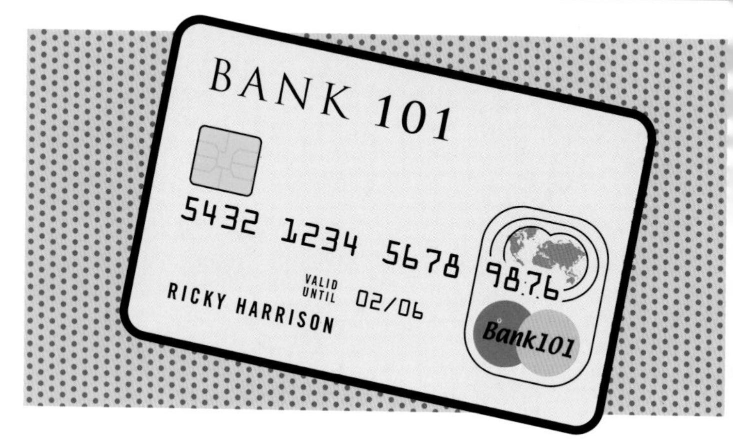

Make at Least One Huge Purchase You Can't Afford

You've agonised about it for ages, you fell in love with it the moment you saw it. You've drooled at the window display, and every time you're in the shop you make a detour to walk past it. It's something that you wouldn't normally buy or can't really afford, your heart says YES!, your bank balance always says NOOOooooo! For some people it's a masterpiece, a lock of hair from their dead idol's head or a menu once looked at by Elvis Presley. For others it's a pair of jeans that shouldn't cost anywhere near that amount, a house or an electric glowing table.

The Realisation

It's too late now; it's in your house and it's too big to move without the aid of professional furniture removers. You did a deal – they let you have it cheaper on condition you can't take it back – you're stuck with it now. What have you done?

The Consequences

The credit card bill. Be prepared for years of credit card interest, but it was worth every penny, wasn't it?

Things to Spend Your Money On ...
A trip of a lifetime, a mansion, a yacht, a supercar, bring Concorde out of retirement and fly it, an island, your children, the ultimate wedding, the ultimate funeral.

Make at Least One Huge Purchase
You Can't Afford **Form**

Once you have completed this **Thing To Do**, stick your Achieved Star here and fill in the form

Achieved

Date of your purchase

d d m m y y y y

What is the item you bought?

Where did you buy the item from?

Tick the corresponding box for the length of time it took you to decide to buy the item?

Years	Weeks	Days	Hours	Minutes	Seconds

Did you pay for the item with a credit card? y/n

How long has it taken you to pay for the item?

Years	Weeks	Days	Hours	Minutes	Seconds

Did you get a discount on the item? y/n

If yes, what percentage? %

Did you have to take out a second credit card to pay for the item? y/n

Are you still paying for the item? y/n

If yes, how much extra interest have you had to pay? THINGS TO DO £/$

Did you get into trouble for buying the item? y/n

If yes, who did you get into trouble with?

Parents	Wife or Husband	Boyfriend or Girlfriend	Your Boss	Bank Manager	Other

If other, please specify

Did you try and take the item back? y/n

Write the total cost of the item in the receipt below

THANK YOU
FOR YOUR CUSTOM
PLEASE CALL AGAIN

Item

Discount %

Cost of item before discount THINGS TO DO £/$

OVERALL TOTAL

At the same time you could complete these **Things To Do**
45: Do a Runner From a Fancy Restaurant • 72: Have Enough Money to Do All the Things on This List • 90: Join the 16-Mile High Club

Score the Winning Goal / Try / Basket*

Has scoring the winner in the last minute of extra time in the World Cup final always been your childhood dream (see **Thing To Do** No. 8)? Well, let's be honest, it still might not happen, but at least you can try and score the winning goal in your Thursday evening five-a-side football grudge match tournaments. They're always closely fought matches and within thirty minutes of playing the score is 16–16; it could be your moment, even if you are the goalie.

We Are the Champions

- Enjoy the moment. Let enjoyment turn into smugness
- The other team members should be made to donate a prize. The prize should be paid in beer
- Never let the other team forget it. Rub in your personal victory at every given opportunity
- Dine on the story of your winning goal for years. Bore the pants off all your family and friends
- Make yourself a trophy to honour the moment

If football isn't your sport, adapt the form to the sport you scored the winner in.

* Delete where applicable

The Ultimate Last Minute Winner The score is 17–17 in the 2003 Rugby World Cup final, extra time is almost over; with only 26 seconds left on the clock, Jonny Wilkinson scores his first drop goal of the match and with it wins the Rugby World Cup for England.

Score the Winning Goal / Try / Basket **Form**

Once you have completed this **Thing To Do**, stick your Achieved Star here and fill in the form

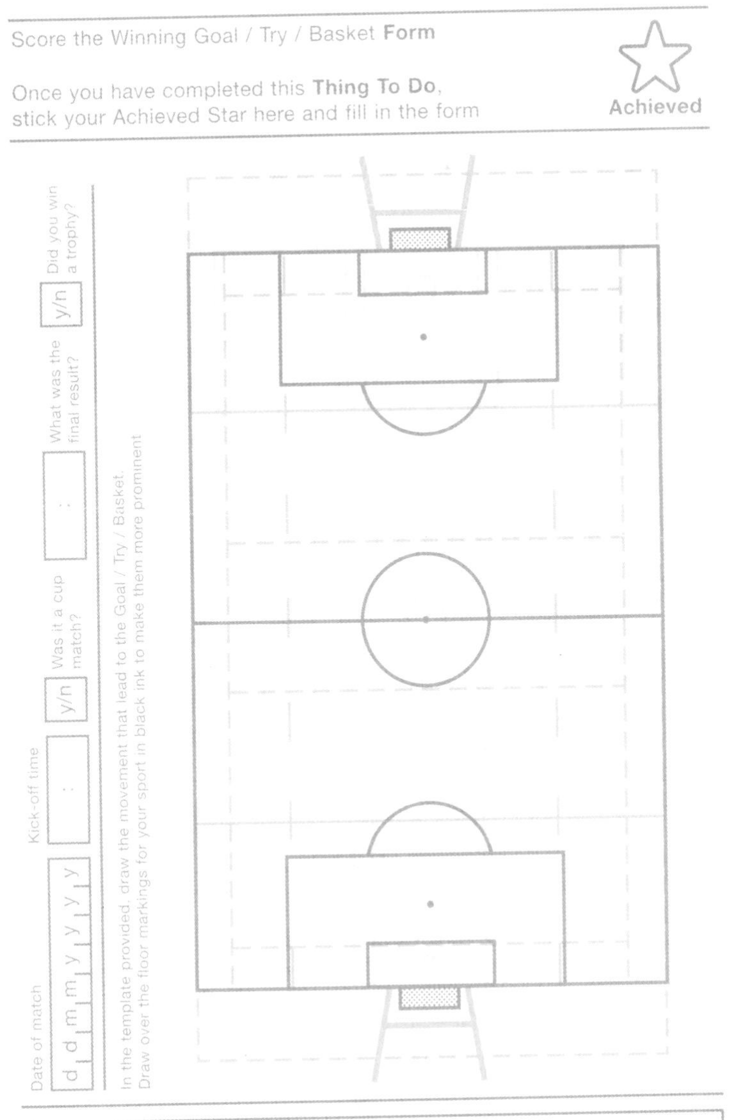

Achieved
Date of match
d d m m y y y y
Kick-off time
:
Was it a cup match?
y/n
What was the final result?
:
Did you win a trophy?
y/n
In the template provided, draw the movement that lead to the Goal / Try / Basket.
Draw over the floor markings for your sport in black ink to make them more prominent

At the same time you could complete these **Things To Do**
03: Win an Award, Trophy or Prize • 48: Be Present When Your Country Wins the World Cup • 65: Shout 'Drinks Are on Me!' in a Pub or a Bar

Where Do You Think You're Going?

Gatecrash a Fancy Party

You've got to get into that party. Free drink, free food and packed to the seams with the rich and famous. You haven't got an invitation because you haven't got anything to do with the party. Put on your favourite outfit and give it your best shot ...

Fight for Your Right to Party

- Via the guest list. If you know of someone else who is going to the party, get there before them and steal their identity. Once inside, keep a low profile as the doormen might try to hunt you down
- Walk straight up to the door confidently, as if you are supposed to be there – they're bound to let you in
- If it's a launch party, claim you're from a national newspaper gossip page

The Great Pretender

- Be anyone you like. If it's a party for a film launch (see **Thing To Do** No. 44), you're an actor; if it's for a new product, you're the genius behind the advertising campaign. Take the credit for everybody else's hard work

The Comedy Terrorist In June 2003, the comedian Aaron Barschak climbed over a wall at Windsor Castle, dressed as Osama bin Laden, and gatecrashed Prince William's 21st birthday party. He managed to get on stage and do part of his routine before he was arrested.

Gatecrash a Fancy Party **Form**

Once you have completed this **Thing To Do**, stick your Achieved Star here and fill in the form

Achieved

Date and time of the party

d d m m y y y y :

Do you know who was hosting the party?

Where was the party?

How did you gatecrash the party?

Used someone else's name | Used someone else's ticket | Walked in unchallenged | Snuck in the back door | Bribery | Other

If other, please clarify

What kind of party was it?

Launch party | Fancy dress | Masked ball | After-show party | Warehouse party | Other

If other, please clarify

If it was fancy dress, what did you go as?

If it was a launch party, did you get a goody bag?

y/n If yes, what was in it?

Was anyone famous there?

y/n If yes, who?

How many of you gatecrashed the party?

Were there free drinks? y/n

If yes, how many did you have?

How would you rate the party?

Excellent | Very Good | Good | OK | Poor

Did anyone realise you shouldn't be there? y/n

If yes, who?

Did you get thrown out? y/n

Explain what happened

At the same time you could complete these **Things To Do**
29: Meet Your Idol • 44: Attend a Film Premiere • 63: Make the Front Page of a National Newspaper • 99: Confess

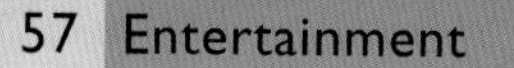

See the All-time Greatest Films

Like the greatest books list (see **Thing To Do** No. 52) there are hundreds of all-time greatest film lists to choose from, although the film list is a lot easier to compile; you have a hundred years of film to choose from rather than centuries of writing.

Compare greatest film lists and they're always pretty similar to each other; they mention the **Usual Suspects** time and time again; some of them we know well, others are **Alien** to us, but the films on the list are all **Shining** examples of the best films. **The Thing** is, you'd be **Unforgiven** for not watching them.

Do the Right Thing and chose a decent film list; here's a collection of films to get you started; some of the films make the greatest films list, the majority of them don't. Some of the films should make the greatest films list and others need to be seen to be believed and then never seen again. If you disagree with this list you're a **Psycho**.

The Lumière Brothers are credited with the birth of film. The first paying audience watched a film through their *cinématographe* device on 28 December 1895. When they showed their film *L'Arrivée d'un train en gare de la Ciotat* (The Arrival of a Train at La Ciotat Station) people fled the cinema, believing the train would come out of the screen.

See the All-time Greatest Films **Form**

X Goonies
X Princess Bride

Once you have completed this **Thing To Do**, stick your Achieved Star here and fill in the form

Achieved

- 12 Angry Men (1957)
- 2001: A Space Odyssey (1968)
- A Bout de Souffle (1959)
- Alien (1979)
- Aliens (1986)
- Amadeus (1984)
- Amelie (2001)
- American Beauty (1999)
- American Werewolf in London, An (1981)
- Annie Hall (1977)
- Apocalypse Now (1979)
- Arsenic and Old Lace (1944)
- Audition (2000)
- Back to the Future (1985)
- Barbarella (1967)
- Big Lebowski, The (1998)
- Big Wednesday (1978)
- Blade Runner (1982)
- Blue Velvet (1985)
- Boot, Das (1981)
- Brazil (1985)
- Breakfast at Tiffany's (1961)
- Breakfast Club, The (1985)
- Butch Cassidy and the Sundance Kid (1969)
- Caddyshack (1980)
- Casablanca (1942)
- Casino (1995)
- Christmas Carol, A / Scrooge (1970)
- Citizen Kane (1941)
- City of God (2002)
- Clash of the Titans (1981)
- Close Encounters of the Third Kind (1977)
- Deer Hunter, The (1978)
- Deliverance (1972)
- Diaboliques, Les (1955)
- Donnie Darko (2001)
- Do the Right Thing (1989)
- Dr Strangelove or: How I Learned to Stop Worrying and Love the Bomb (1964)
- Ed Wood (1994)
- Elephant Man, The (1980)
- Empire Strikes Back, The (1980)
- Enter the Dragon (1973)
- Eraserhead (1977)
- Evil Dead 2 (1987)
- Ferris Bueller's Day Off (1986)
- Festen (1998)
- Fight Club (1999)
- Flash Gordon (1980)
- Ghostbusters (1984)
- Godfather: Part 1, The (1972)
- Godfather: Part 2, The (1974)
- Good, the Bad and the Ugly, The (1966)
- Goodfellas (1990)
- Graduate, The (1967)
- Great Escape, The (1962)
- Grosse Point Blank (1997)
- Groundhog Day (1993)
- Harold and Maude (1971)
- Harvey (1950)
- Heathers (1989)
- Italian Job, The (1969)
- It's a Wonderful Life (1946)
- Jaws (1975)
- Jules et Jim (1962)
- Jungle Book, The (1967)
- Kind Hearts and Coronets (1949)
- Kingpin (1996)
- L.A. Confidential (1997)
- Ladykillers, The (1955)
- Lord of the Rings, The Fellowship of the Ring, The (2001)
- Lost in Translation (2003)
- Matrix, The (1999)
- Memento (2000)
- Monty Python and the Holy Grail (1975)
- Monty Python's Life of Brian (1979)
- National Lampoon's Animal House (1978)
- Night of the Hunter, The (1955)
- North by Northwest (1959)
- O Brother, Where Art Thou? (2000)
- Omen, The (1976)
- One Flew Over the Cuckoo's Nest (1975)
- Passage to India, A (1984)
- Peeping Tom (1960)
- Pi (1998)
- Pirates of the Caribbean: The Curse of the Black Pearl (2003)
- Planes, Trains and Automobiles (1987)
- Platoon (1986)
- Producers, The (1967)
- Psycho (1960)
- Pulp Fiction (1994)
- Raiders of the Lost Ark (1981)
- Rear Window (1954)
- Right Stuff, The (1983)
- Ring, The (2002)
- Risky Business (1983)
- Royal Tenenbaums, The (2001)
- Scanners (1981)
- Secretary (2002)
- Sexy Beast (2000)
- Se7en (1995)
- Seven Samurai (1954)
- Shawshank Redemption, The (1994)
- Shining, The (1980)
- Shrek (2001)
- Sixth Sense, The (1999)
- Spirited Away (2001)
- Star Wars (1977)
- Sting, The (1973)
- Straight Story, The (1999)
- Sure Thing, The (1985)
- Swingers (1996)
- Taxi Driver (1976)
- Terminator 2: Judgement Day (1991)
- Texas Chainsaw Massacre, The (1974)
- Thing, The (1982)
- This Is Spinal Tap (1983)
- To Kill a Mockingbird (1962)
- Top Secret! (1984)
- Touch of Evil (1958)
- Toy Story (1995)
- Toy Story 2 (1999)
- Trading Places (1983)
- True Romance (1993)
- Two-Lane Blacktop (1971)
- Untouchables, The (1987)
- Usual Suspects, The (1995)
- Vanishing, The (1988)
- Videodrome (1982)
- When We Were Kings (1996)
- Wicker Man, The (1973)
- Withnail & I (1987)
- Young Frankenstein (1974)

At the same time you could complete these **Things To Do**

29: Meet Your Idol • 44: Attend a Film Premiere

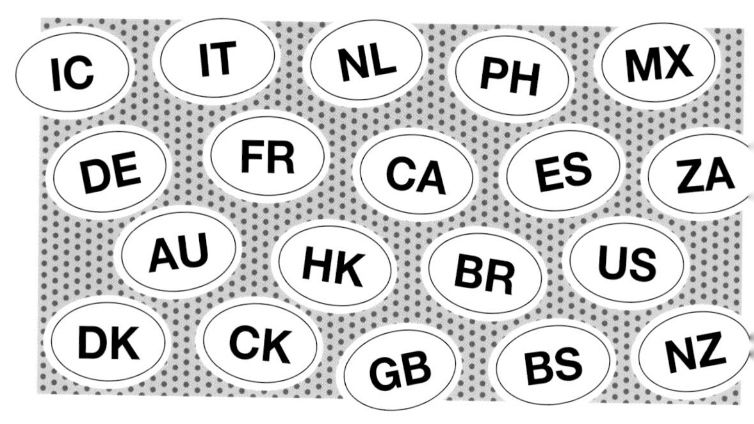

Live in the Place You Love

On your travels around the world (see **Thing To Do** No. 36) you'll fall in love with hundreds of places. It is one of the best things about going on holiday, taking in the sights and sounds and getting away from it all. But why not get away from it all for ever? Give up the job you've hated for years (see **Thing To Do** No. 59), pack up your personal possessions, seek out the sun, sea and hot weather, and live in the place you love.

With plenty of towns, cities and places the world over, there is always going to be somewhere out there that you feel an affinity for. Choose a destination where your hard-earned cash will stretch twice as far as it does in your own country.

Move to a deserted island and build a bar on it. The ultimate desert island, surrounded by blue sea and sand, free of everything except trees, rocks, beer and bar snacks. Your life will become completely stress free and the only worry you'll have is whether the boat delivering the beer will sink or not.

Other Places You Could Live In your favourite pub or bar • In your childhood home • In the place where you were born • In the country • In the city • In the hills • In the wilderness • In solitude • In a commune • On a boat • In a van

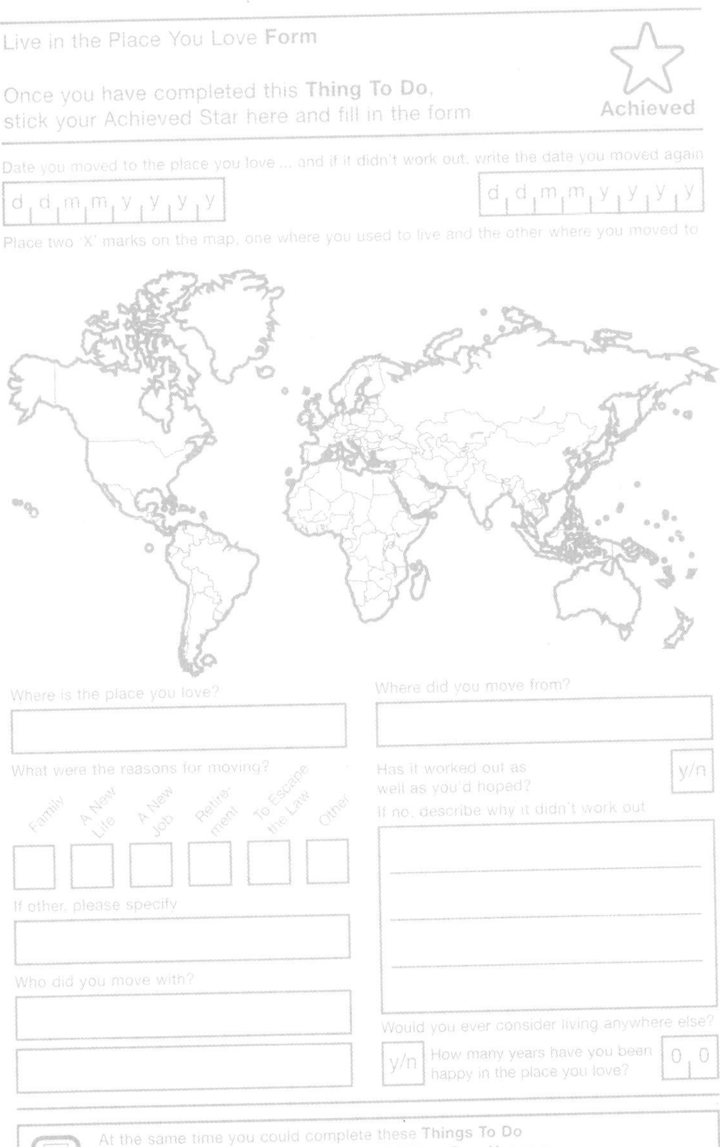

Live in the Place You Love **Form**

Once you have completed this **Thing To Do**, stick your Achieved Star here and fill in the form

Achieved

Date you moved to the place you love ... and if it didn't work out, write the date you moved again

d d m m y y y y

d d m m y y y y

Place two 'X' marks on the map, one where you used to live and the other where you moved to

Where is the place you love?

Where did you move from?

What were the reasons for moving?

Family | A New Life | A New Job | Retirement | To Escape the Law | Other

If other, please specify

Who did you move with?

Has it worked out as well as you'd hoped? y/n

If no, describe why it didn't work out

Would you ever consider living anywhere else? y/n

How many years have you been happy in the place you love? 0 0

At the same time you could complete these **Things To Do**
51: Learn Another Language • 82: Build Your Own House • 97: Live Out of a Van • 100: Reach 100 Years of Age

* Draw in boss's reaction

Step 1: Leave a Job You Hate

Even the best jobs can turn sour, and at some stage of their working life, most people will find themselves stuck in a job they hate. The easy part is to get stuck in a rut, the hard part is to get up and leave. But don't sit and suffer. Quit! Leave in style! You'll feel great and the rest of the office will talk about it for years. You'll be a hero.

Step 2: Realisation

You've talked about it for months and you've threatened to leave on previous occasions but never went through with it. Nobody thought you'd ever leave but finally you have. You've done it! Give yourself a month off to do the things you always wanted to do or just chill out. You've earned it.

Step 3: Revenge

Now the fun part: time to get your own back. The best revenge is to start your own company, in direct competition with your old employers if possible. If this isn't possible join a competitor. Either way, remember to take the client list from your old job, the one that you've compiled over all those unhappy months. It might just come in handy.

Always snub the attempts of your former employer to go out for drinks. They didn't value you when you were around, so why value them now?
Never go back on your decision. Remember, the company will fall apart without you.

Leave a Job You Hate **Form**

Once you have completed this **Thing To Do**,
stick your Achieved Star here and fill in the form

Name of company

Name of your boss

How long were you with the company?

Years Months

Was the job enjoyable at the start?

y/n If no, why did you stay?

Reasons for leaving

Was an insult used?

y/n If yes, which one?

If verbal, please clarify:

Do you agree with the statements? Choose an answer from 1 to 5, 1 being the lowest and 5 being the highest. **Do you feel you were**

Undervalued?

1 2 3 4 5

Underpaid?

1 2 3 4 5

Overworked?

1 2 3 4 5

Blamed for others' mistakes?

1 2 3 4 5

Having to cover for other people's laziness?

1 2 3 4 5

Bullied?

1 2 3 4 5

Getting nowhere fast?

1 2 3 4 5

Bored?

1 2 3 4 5

What have you been doing since you left the job?

At the same time you could complete these **Things To Do**
10: Leave Your Mark in Graffiti • 23: Get Arrested • 36: Visit Every Country • 95: Get Revenge

Take Part in a Police Line-up

If you didn't do the crime you've got nothing to worry about. It's a great way to earn some extra cash, you'll be provided with complimentary tea and biscuits and if you're up to it, have a laugh at the expense of the police at the same time.

How to Be Positively Identified in Police Line-up

- Dress in a stripy jumper and balaclava or ski mask
- Look shifty, suspicious and guilty
- When the victim comes into the room, brag loudly about other crimes you've committed
- Develop a nervous twitch
- Have a plastic gun poking out the top of your jeans
- If you're asked to read out a statement, say 'He made me do it' instead of reading the statement on the card and point at the person standing next to you
- Cover your face with your hands the entire length of the parade
- Wear a T-shirt with 'I did it' printed on it
- Face the wall

Make sure you haven't committed the crime that you're in the line-up for.

In Case of Accidental Arrest
Know your rights, practise escapology from handcuffs, practise lock-picking, learn to hide items on your person where the police won't find them, stay away from the big guys.

Take Part in a Police Line-up **Form**

Once you have completed this **Thing To Do**, stick your Achieved Star here and fill in the form

Achieved

Date and time of the line-up

d d m m y y y y | :

Where was the line-up held?

What was the crime that the line-up was for?

Did you get paid? y/n If yes, how much? THINGS TO DO £/$

How long did it take? hrs

How many people were there in the line-up?

Which position were you in the line-up?

Did you have to read a statement? y/n If yes, what did you have to say?

y/n Did you all have to dress the same?

y/n Was the victim behind one way glass?

y/n Did you get picked out as the chief suspect?

y/n Were you in the line-up because you committed the crime?

Where were you in relation to the suspect? Write in your position in the line-up. Tick the box to show where you were and mark the suspect with a cross

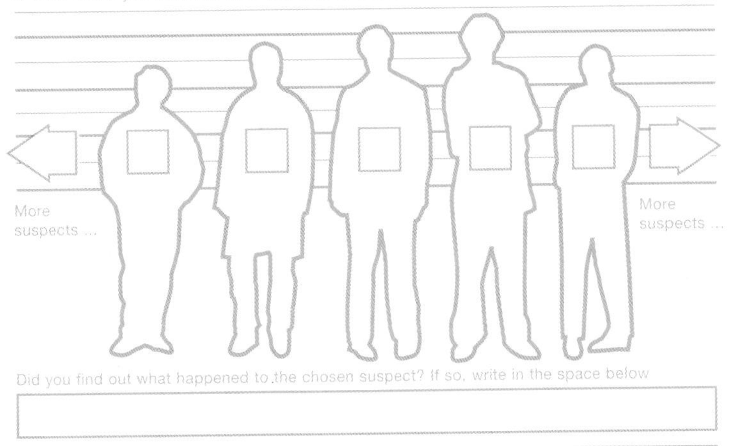

Did you find out what happened to the chosen suspect? If so, write in the space below

At the same time you could complete these **Things To Do**
23: Get Arrested • 61: Get Away with the Perfect Practical Joke or Hoax • 99: Confess

Get Away with the Perfect Practical Joke or Hoax

Why confine pranks to April Fools' Day? Surely every month should have its fair share of practical jokes. To get away with the best practical joke you've got to think of something that can't be topped and it's got to be something that is simple but jaw-droppingly brilliant. All the time, money and effort you put into the prank will be repaid tenfold with the look of horror on your victim's face.

If you find yourself looking after a friend's place, fill their house from top to bottom with popcorn or cover everything they own in aluminium foil. A couple on their way back from honeymoon might come back home to a boarded-up house and 'Crime scene – Do not enter' tape. They might already have been stopped at customs for the gun shape you cut out of metal, which appeared on the x-ray machine. After all, what are best friends for?

You Don't Fool Me

- Make sure your victim has a good sense of humour
- Be careful of retaliation; don't go too far, it could end in tears
- If your victim does manage to get their own back, you've got to go one better again. Keep this up until they back down and you win

April Fools' Day With the introduction of the Gregorian Calendar in 1582, New Year's Day, originally celebrated on 1 April, was moved to 1 January. In France, many people didn't accept the change and continued their celebrations on 1 April. They were ridiculed.

Get Away With the Perfect Practical Joke or Hoax **Form**

Once you have completed this **Thing To Do**, stick your Achieved Star here and fill in the form

Achieved

The Perfect Joke

Date and time of your practical joke

d d m m y y y y :

Who were your victim(s)?

Describe your perfect practical joke

Did it go as planned? y/n

If no, what went wrong?

On a scale from 1 to 10 how well did the joke go?

1 2 3 4 5 6 7 8 9 10

Did your victim take it well? y/n

Did your victim utter the words 'Just you wait, I'll get you back!'? y/n

The Perfect Hoax

Date and time of your hoax

d d m m y y y y :

Who were your victim(s)?

Describe your perfect hoax

Did it go as planned? y/n

If no, what went wrong?

On a scale from 1 to 10 how well did the hoax go?

1 2 3 4 5 6 7 8 9 10

Did you manage to fool the newspapers? y/n

If yes, how long for? Weeks Days

At the same time you could complete these **Things To Do**
10: Leave Your Mark in Graffiti • 23: Get Arrested •
60: Take Part in a Police Line-up • 91: Publish a Cult Website

Join the Mile High Club

10% of us claim to have joined the mile high club and another 50% of us want to. To qualify, you just need to have sex at more than 5,280ft (1 mile) in the air.

The best time to achieve this during your flight is about 20 minutes into the inflight film, then you can both sneak off to the toilets, or ideally, if your flight is an overnight one, when the cabin lights have gone down and everyone is sleeping. Alternatively, learn to fly a plane (see **Thing To Do** No. 74) and you're in complete control of where and when, or rather your auto-pilot is. You could attempt it with a stewardess – it'd give a new meaning to 'Thank you for flying with us, we hope to see you again soon'.

In Your Seat

- Don't give your blankets away to anyone, you're going to need them

In the toilet

- Be careful not to press the call button with your knee or an elbow or anything else
- Be quick. If you're in the toilets for over 15 minutes, the stewards are entitled to open the door to check that the occupant is OK

The First Mile-highers Lawrence Sperry (an ace pilot and the inventor of the auto-pilot) and Mrs Waldo Polk. In 1916, while giving flying lessons in his flying boat, the plane crashed. They were discovered alive and naked in the South Bay, New York.

Join the Mile High Club **Form**

Once you have completed this **Thing To Do**, stick your Achieved Star here and fill in the form

Achieved

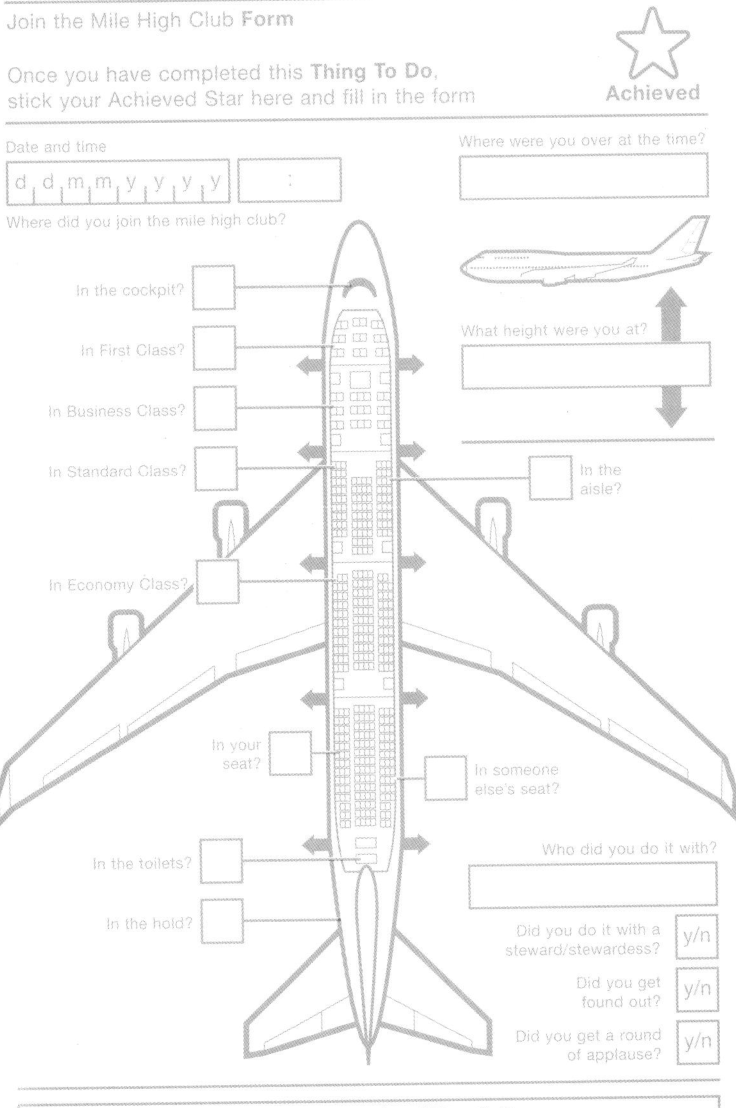

Date and time
d d m m y y y y
:
Where were you over at the time?
Where did you join the mile high club?
In the cockpit?
In First Class?
In Business Class?
In Standard Class?
In Economy Class?
What height were you at?
In the aisle?
In your seat?
In someone else's seat?
In the toilets?
In the hold?
Who did you do it with?
Did you do it with a steward/stewardess?
y/n
Did you get found out?
y/n
Did you get a round of applause?
y/n

At the same time you could complete these **Things To Do**
18: Study the *Kama Sutra* and Put Theory into Practice • 23: Get Arrested • 40: Get a Free Upgrade on a Plane

Make the Front Page of a National Newspaper

There are plenty of ways to get yourself onto the front of a national newspaper, but these days it's usually through scandal, disaster or murder. If you want to make the headlines and you don't want it to be for any of these reasons, it's going to take something pretty inventive to push these topics aside for your story.

Local newspapers are a much easier proposition. In some parts of the country, 'Cat caught in tree' or 'Lorry mounts kerb' still make it onto the front of newspapers ... Surely you can do much better than that.

Read All About It

- Become famous – some papers will report anything and everything you do
- Become a huge lottery winner – say things like 'it won't change me' and 'I'll keep my day job'
- Pick your day carefully; if a huge story comes along, your effort will be pushed off the front page
- Dish the dirt – become a world exclusive, kiss and tell on someone famous
- Pull off a hoax that fools everyone, especially the newspaper it's printed in

Famous Hoaxes
The 1967 Bluff Creek Bigfoot footage • The 62 volumes of Hitler's diaries that surfaced in 1983 • Ray Santilli's Roswell Alien Autopsy film • Crop circles

Make the Front Page of a
National Newspaper **Form**
Once you have completed this **Thing To Do**,
stick your Achieved Star here and fill in the form

Newspaper masthead here

day | d d m m y y y y | price

Write your headline here

Write the article here

Write the article here, write the article here, write the article here.

Write the article in here, write the article in here, write the article in here, write the article in here, write the article in here, write the article in here, write the article in here, write the article in here, write the article.
Write the article in here, write the article in here, write the article in here, write the article in here, write the article in here, write the article in here, write the article in here, write the article in here, write the article.
Write the article in here, write the article in here, write the

Was there a photo of you on the front page? If yes, place it here

Photo caption here

Continue the article here

article in here, write the article in here, write the article in here, write the article in here, write the article in here, write the article in here, write the article in here, write the article in here, write the article in here, write the article in here.

At the same time you could complete these **Things To Do**
03: Win an Award, Trophy or Prize • 05: Make a Discovery • 23: Get Arrested • 29: Meet Your Idol • 44: Attend a Film Premiere

Drive a Car at Top Speed

We all speed without even thinking about it but it's those speeding tickets that soon bring us back to a snail's pace. If you feel the need for speed you could try driving your car at top speed on the motorway in the dead of night but this early morning behaviour will only attract the attention of the cops and within minutes they'll have cars, motorbikes and a helicopter chasing you; you know it's a matter of time before you get caught. Stick to driving fast in driving school cars this way you won't get stopped for speeding; if you wreck the car you can walk away from it without a ridiculous repair bill to pay and drive off in your own scratch-free car. More importantly, you've got a better, faster choice of vehicle to drive than your own; it's your way of playing at being a racing driver, even if it is only for a day.

Driven by You

- **Formula 1** – 0–100mph in 3.6 seconds
- **Formula 3** – a scaled-down Formula 1 car capable of 165mph
- **Rally Car** – Tear around dirt tracks and courses that you wouldn't attempt in your own car
- **Supercars** – Drive the car you've always wanted to. Take a Ferrari for a spin and race it against a Porsche
- **Motorbikes** – Deathtraps

Boy Racers The autobahns in Germany have no speed limit, you can easily travel at 200mph if your car can go that fast. Always keep an eye on your mirrors, one minute there's nothing behind you, next minute you've got a world speed record attempt on your tail.

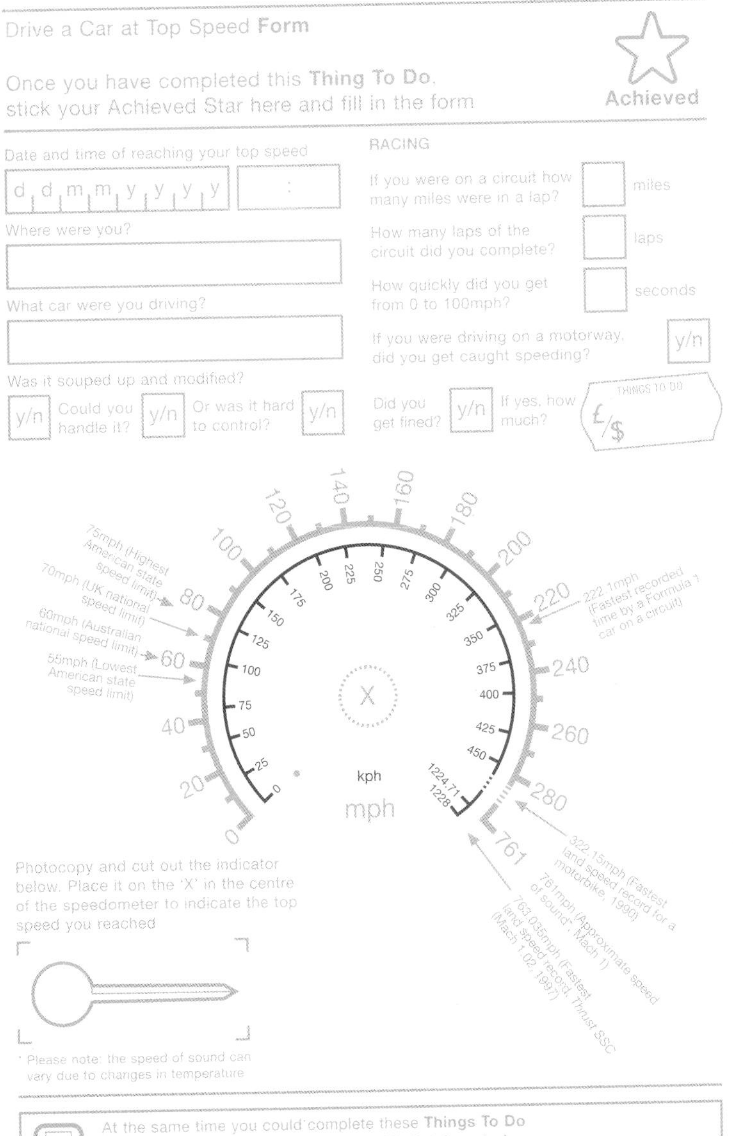
Drive a Car at Top Speed **Form**

Once you have completed this **Thing To Do**, stick your Achieved Star here and fill in the form

Achieved

Date and time of reaching your top speed

d d m m y y y y :

Where were you?

What car were you driving?

Was it souped up and modified? y/n Could you handle it? y/n Or was it hard to control? y/n

RACING

If you were on a circuit how many miles were in a lap? miles

How many laps of the circuit did you complete? laps

How quickly did you get from 0 to 100mph? seconds

If you were driving on a motorway, did you get caught speeding? y/n

Did you get fined? y/n If yes, how much? £/$

Photocopy and cut out the indicator below. Place it on the 'X' in the centre of the speedometer to indicate the top speed you reached

* Please note: the speed of sound can vary due to changes in temperature

At the same time you could complete these **Things To Do**
03: Win an Award, Trophy or Prize • 23: Get Arrested • 43: Throw a Dart into a Map and Travel to Where it Lands

Shout 'Drinks Are on Me!' in a Pub or a Bar

It seems to happen every day in film or on TV; there is always someone getting a free drink for the feeblest of reasons, but in real life it just doesn't happen. Free drinks are handed out as if they're sweets on TV but 'Drinks are on me!' is never shouted in a real pub situation. It's a myth, like babies' pee being blue in adverts or that cooking really is that simple. It's time to turn fiction into fact. Shout 'Drinks are on me!' in your local and become everybody's new best friend.

You're My Best Friend

- Chose a quiet weeknight in the local pub
- Make sure the majority of the crowd are your friends
- Make sure everybody only has one drink each otherwise they'll take advantage and drink you dry
- Make sure you have enough money to cover the bill
- Think of an outlandish reason for your generous act; when asked why you bought everyone drinks say 'We are the Champions' (but don't explain of what), 'I'm the landlord' or 'Because my horoscope told me to'

So, why do it? Because you're feeling flush, you've had some great news or maybe you've already had too much beer ...

Drinks Are on Them
Make a bet with the landlord of the pub. Make sure it's a bet you can win, make the outcome of the bet free drinks for the rest of your life. Win the bet.

Shout 'Drinks Are on Me!' in a Pub or a Bar **Form**

Once you have completed this **Thing To Do**, stick your Achieved Star here and fill in the form

Achieved

Date and time of your announcement

d d m m y y y y :

Where were you?

Why did you shout 'Drinks are on me!'? Because ...

- You've come into money
- You were drunk
- You're getting married
- This book
- You're having a baby
- Other

If other, please clarify

On hearing the news, what response did you get?

Cheering | Applause | Heckling | Whistling | Bottle-throwing | Other

If other, please clarify

Was everyone your best friend that night? y/n

Did you talk to people you'd usually avoid? y/n

What did you tell people was the reason for your announcement?

Would you do it again? y/n

THANK YOU

FOR YOUR CUSTOM
PLEASE CALL AGAIN

List the drinks and the amounts you bought

TOTAL

At the same time you could complete these **Things To Do**

72: Have Enough Money to Do All the Things on This List •
93: Complete the Monopoly Board Pub Crawl

Be Part of a Flash Mob

Flash mobbing started during the summer of 2003 and it quickly became a worldwide phenomenon. It's basically an excuse for members of the public to act stupid simultaneously for the bemused enjoyment of passers-by.

Flash Mobbing
A seemingly coincidental convergence of people who participate in a bizarre activity, then disappear.

Flash

- To the outsider it appears that the flash mob members converge from nowhere, a completely unplanned and spontaneous meeting; in reality, the time, date and an outline of the event is predetermined and sent by email. At a given moment, the group will take part in a mass event; it could be anything from waving bananas or shouting 'Ahoy!' at passing boats, anything as long as it's silly and pointless. Whatever it is, as soon as it's over everyone disperses, and within moments it's as if nothing happened

Flash Mob, a History The first flash mob took place in the rug department store in Macy's, New York City. 100 people gathered round a 'love rug'; they told the staff they lived in a carpet warehouse commune. Then they all disappeared again.

Be Part of a Flash Mob **Form**

Once you have completed this **Thing To Do**, stick your Achieved Star here and fill in the form

Achieved

Draw in the spaces below what happened during the flash mobbing or place photos of yourself in mid mob

Gathering

:

Mobbing

:

Was anything said? If yes, write in the bubble

Dispersion

:

Date of flash mobbing

d d m m y y y y

Place of flash mobbing

How did you find out about the flash mob?

How many people were involved?

What was the total time of the flash mobbing?

Minutes Seconds

Were props used? y/n

If yes, what were they?

Explain what happened

At the same time you could complete these **Things To Do**
43: Throw a Dart into a Map and Travel to Where it Lands • 56: Gatecrash a Fancy Party 61: Get Away with the Perfect Practical Joke or Hoax • 67: Visit ...

Visit ...

As you embark on your epic journey around the world, visiting every country (See **Thing To Do** No. 36), there is plenty of time to stop and take in the sights ...

Here are twelve of the most famous world sites to visit.

Remember to take your camera and camcorder with you everywhere, the basic equipment of a tourist. If you want to go unnoticed among the other tourists remember to dress the same as everyone else and hang around in a big group following a lady with her umbrella in the air.

Regulation tourist attire and equipment

- A bum bag or fanny pack, filled to capacity
- A plastic see-through rain mac for all weather
- Shorts in winter, trousers in summer
- Brightly coloured clothes
- Ill-fitting open-toed sandals

Other places to visit ...

Iguacu Falls
An enormous series of waterfalls 36 times larger than Niagra Falls on the Brazil–Argentina border

Yosemite National Park
An area of natural beauty crammed full with wild animals for over 1,000 square miles

Iceland
The land of fire and ice with its volcanos, geysers, hot springs and plenty of snow and ice

The Galapagos Islands
These unspoilt islands are the best place to swim and commune with nature

Stonehenge
England's most famous stone circle, constructed over 4,000 years ago

Don't be afraid to ask a fellow tourist to take a photograph of you and your partner. If a tourist asks you the same request, happily oblige. They won't know you've chopped their heads out of the picture until they get the photographs developed.

Visit ... **Form**

Once you have completed this **Thing To Do**, stick your Achieved Star here and fill in the form

Achieved

Colosseum, Rome
d d m m y y y y

Uluru, Australia
d d m m y y y y

Machu Picchu, Peru
d d m m y y y y

The Pyramids at Giza, Egypt
d d m m y y y y

Christ the Redeemer, Rio de Janeiro
d d m m y y y y

Sydney Harbour, Australia
d d m m y y y y

Taj Mahal, Delhi
d d m m y y y y

Great Barrier Reef, Australia
d d m m y y y y

Golden Gate Bridge, San Francisco
d d m m y y y y

Grand Canyon, Arizona
d d m m y y y y

Angkor Wat, Cambodia
d d m m y y y y

The Great Wall of China
d d m m y y y y

At the same time you could complete these **Things To Do**
30: Stay in the Best Suite in a Five Star Hotel • 36: Visit Every Country
62: Join the Mile High Club • 58: Live in the Place You Love

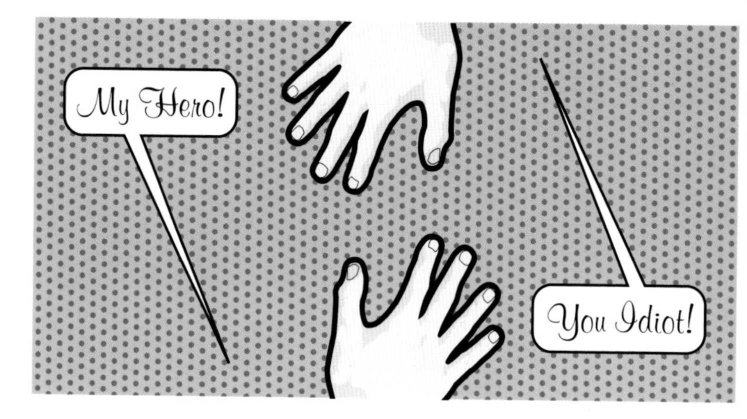

Save Someone's Life

The ultimate sacrifice giving your life to save others. But hold on, it may be the ultimate thing to do but face it, you want to get out of this alive and hopefully with a few medals to confirm your brave act; besides, how can you fill out the **Thing To Do** form if you're dead?

I Will Survive

- Become a nurse, a doctor or a surgeon, you'll save lives every day. Become a lifeguard and be ready to save a life at a moment's notice

- Become the safety officer at your work, learn the safety drills and how to correctly perform CPR; you never know who's going to drop dead in front of you in the bus queue

- Perfect the Heimlich Manoeuvre, a very handy life-saving technique to know. It can be used in restaurants, cafes and bars; just add food

- Put someone into a life-threatening situation without them knowing, then save them from that situation. IMPORTANT: whatever you do, save them; otherwise you'll be charged with murder

Save Someone's Life Without Knowing It
Give blood. The average body holds 5 litres of blood; give some of your excess to those who really need it. Donate 475ml, just under a pint. 3 times a year.

Save Someone's Life **Form**

Once you have completed this **Thing To Do**, stick your Achieved Star here and fill in the form

Achieved

Date you saved someone's life

d d m m y y y y

Whose life did you save?

How did you save them?

- Saved them from drowning
- Performed the Heimlich Manoeuvre
- Pulled them from a burning building
- Treated an injury
- Performed CPR
- Donated something
- Actions during a war
- Other

If other, please specify

Did you act instinctively? y/n

Explain what happened

Did you put your own life in danger? y/n

Did you receive any medals for your actions? y/n

If yes, which medals?

Are you still in touch with the person you saved? y/n

Did you appear in the newspaper or on the TV? y/n

If yes, where?

Would you do it again? y/n

Your Life

Has your life been saved? y/n

If yes, explain what happened

Professional Lifesavers

Does your job involve saving lives for a living? y/n

If yes, are you a ...

- Doctor
- Nurse
- Surgeon
- GP
- Fireman
- Paramedic
- Lifeguard
- Other

If other, please specify

How long have you been in your profession?

years

How many lives do you think you've saved?

Have you received awards for your actions? y/n

If yes, what have you received?

Giving Blood

Have you ever given blood? y/n

If yes, how many times?

At the same time you could complete these **Things To Do**
3: Win an Award, Trophy or Prize • 63: Make the Front Page of a National Newspaper • 94: Get Something Named After You

In Various Languages, Learn to ...

If you haven't mastered another language yet (see **Thing To Do** No. 51), at least learn to say the following important words and phrases.

Say Hello, Goodbye, Please and Thank You

Obvious, yes, but if you're polite from the beginning you can progress to more important matters, such as ordering beer.

... Order Beer

A necessary antidote to bus tours, cathedrals and museums. But if the landlord thinks you've had too much, beer will help with the next topic ...

... Swear

Foreign swear words come in handy even if you're in your own country. If being polite or swearing hasn't got you what you want, try ...

... Insults

Learn the worst insult for the country you're in. You'll need to know these phrases for when you're driving around Italy's roads or France's roundabouts. Remember to insult the driver and their mother.

Other Phrases to Learn
'Do you know the way to ...?', 'How much is this?', 'Can you call an ambulance?', 'I'm allergic to ...', 'Help!', 'I didn't do it!', 'I'd like to speak to my lawyer'.

In Various Languages, Learn to ... Form
Once you have completed this Thing To Do, stick your Achieved Star here and fill in the form
Achieved

Write the phrases in the bubbles provided, once you have mastered them

At the same time you could complete these **Things To Do**
51: Learn Another Language • 36: Visit Every Country • 65: Shout 'Drinks Are on Me!' in a Pub or a Bar • 67: Visit ... • 97: Live Out of a Van

Invent a Word That Makes it into the Dictionary

Neologism
A recently coined word or phrase

It's easy to make up a new word but getting them acknowledged in the dictionary is the hard part. It takes a whole nation to adopt the new word before it will make an appearance. At the end of each year a list of new words is announced of the new entries which are going to appear in the next edition of the dictionary. Here are a few examples of words that you might see in a dictionary near you soon:

Bushism
A term to describe the many mis-statements of George W. Bush; see the Bushism '**Misunderestimate**'

Anticipointment
The build-up to eventual disappointment

Giraffiti
Graffiti painted in a high place

Manny
A male nanny

Toxic Bachelor
A single male, afraid to commit

Digitalia
A collection of computer equipment

Insania
Madness on an unparalleled scale

Literary Wordsmiths Shakespeare is credited with inventing over 1,700 words that are still in use today and Charles Dickens is responsible for the phase 'Merry Christmas'; it hadn't been used until his novel *A Christmas Carol* in 1843.

Invent a Word That Makes it into the Dictionary **Form**

Once you have completed this **Thing To Do**, stick your Achieved Star here and fill in the form

Achieved

Date you found your word in the dictionary

d d m m y y y y

Which dictionary did you find your word in?

Did you get a mention for coining the phrase / word? y/n

If you didn't, who did?

How did you invent your word?

Does a picture accompany your word? y/n

Which page did you find it on?

Your word

Pronunciation / /

Definition as it appears in the dictionary

Was the definition of your word correct in the dictionary? y/n

If the definition of your word is wrong in the dictionary, write below the correct meaning

At the same time you could complete these **Things To Do**

51: Learn Another Language • 69: In Various Languages, Learn to ...

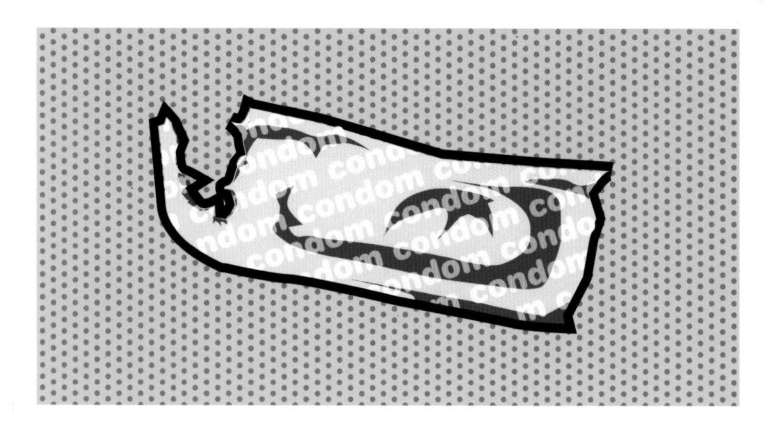

Have Adventurous Sex

Why confine yourself to the bedroom when there is a whole world out there to have sex in.

Taking a risk and the possibility of getting caught in the act is half the fun. Here are nine places to get caught out.

Sex on the beach. Best reserved for those romantic holidays. Make sure you've drunk plenty of cocktails by the same name and don't choose a beach made of pebbles.

At work. Working late is the best excuse to be in the office after hours. Make sure your colleagues have left the building and you've manufactured a huge accident in another part of the building to keep the cleaners busy.

Somewhere inappropriate. This could be anywhere, on the eighteenth green of a golf course or in a churchyard perhaps? Anywhere that would disgust your relatives.

Other Inappropriate Suggestions

- ☐ In a Park
- ☐ On the Stairs
- ☐ In Your Parents' Bed
- ☐ At a Concert
- ☐ In a Penthouse
- ☐ In a Cinema
- ☐ At a Drive-in Movie
- ☐ In a Tent
- ☐ With Someone You Shouldn't
- ☐ In a Swimming Pool
- ☐ At a Party
- ☐ On the Roof
- ☐ In a Churchyard
- ☐ In a Limousine

Have Sex Under the Aurora Borealis The oldest records on the Aurora Borealis, from 2,600BC read 'Fu-Pao, the mother of the Yellow Empire Shuan-Yuan, saw strong lightning moving around the star Su, which belongs to the constellation of Bei-Dou, and the light illuminated the whole area. After that she became pregnant'.

Have Adventurous **Form**

Once you have completed this **Thing To Do**, stick your Achieved Star here and fill in the form

Achieved

... In a taxi or public transport

d d m m y y y y

Where were you?

... Under the stars

d d m m y y y y

Where were you?

... On camera

d d m m y y y y

Who were you with?

... On the beach

d d m m y y y y

Who were you with?

... In an elevator

1 2 3 4 5 6 B 7 G

d d m m y y y y

Which floors were you between?

... At work

STATIONERY CUPBOARD

d d m m y y y y

Which floor were you on?

... As someone else

d d m m y y y y

Who were you?

... In the middle of nowhere

You are here

d d m m y y y y

Where were you?

... Somewhere inappropriate

18

d d m m y y y y

Where were you?

At the same time you could complete these **Things To Do**
18: Study the *Kama Sutra* and Put Theory into Practice • 20: Get Backstage and Get Off with a Rock God • 30: Stay in the Best Suite in a Five Star Hotel

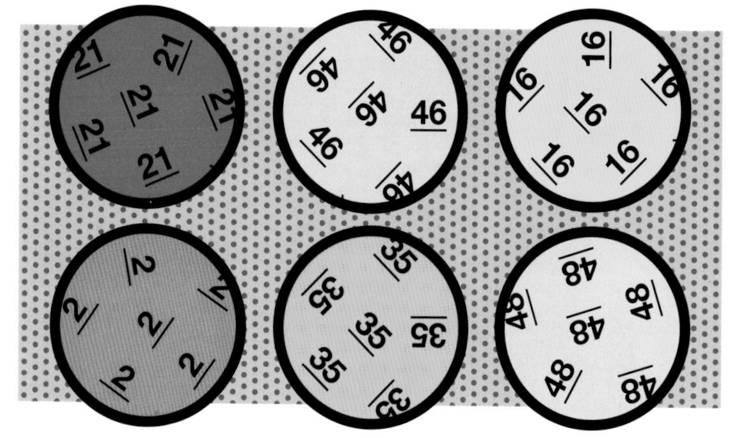

Have Enough Money to Do All the Things on This List

Their are hundreds of ways to earn enough money to do all the things on this list, and many of those already feature on the list. **Things To Do** such as invent something, master poker and win big in a casino, write a best-seller and win an award, trophy or prize could get you the amount you need (see **Things To Do** Nos. 76, 19, 1 and 3).

But if you think you already have enough money to do all the things mentioned on the list, then you'll need an estimated amount of ten million. This figure takes into account the cost of all the flights around the world that you'll need to make, hotel bills, the cost of taking part in all the adventure sports, building your own house and all the other activities that will cost a fortune, like experiencing weightlessness in the zero g plane (see **Things To Do** Nos. 36, 28, 82 and 31). It doesn't end there: the cost could rise even more; it all depends on how much you paid for the item you couldn't afford (see **Things To Do** No. 54) and owning that piece of art can't have been cheap (see **Thing To Do** No. 92).

I Want It All

- If you have got the money, just enjoy it, forget the pension and the kids, spend any inheritance on all the things in this book; after all, you earned it

The Richest Person in the World Bill Gates, the founder of Microsoft. At present he is worth over $40 billion. He earns roughly $5 million a day, which works out to about $60 every second. He has been at the top of the richest person in the world list for the last ten years.

Have Enough Money to Do All the Things on This List **Form**

Once you have completed this **Thing To Do**, stick your Achieved Star here and fill in the form

Achieved

Do you have enough money to do everything on the list? If yes, stick a sticker on the star and revel in the fact that you are incredibly rich. Once you've finished feeling smug carry on through the list

At the same time you could complete these **Things To Do**

30: Stay in the Best Suite in a Five Star Hotel • 31: Experience Weightlessness • 90: Join the 16-Mile High Club • 92: Own an Original Work of Art

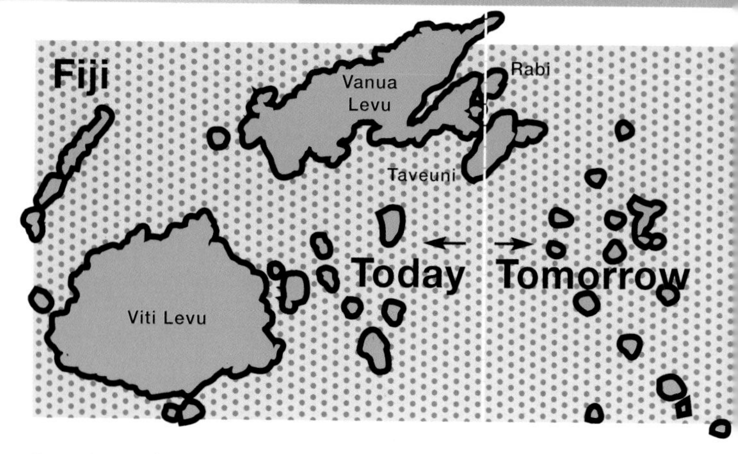

Stand on the International Date Line

The international date line is an imaginary line that runs down the Earth's longitude of 180°. It starts at the North Pole and continues down between Russia and Alaska, down the centre of the Pacific Ocean until it reaches the South Pole in Antarctica. The route for the date line was chosen because the majority of the area covered by the line is ocean; even so the line isn't entirely straight, it fluctuates around groups of islands to keep them within the same time frame, but there is a place where the line does cross land.

On the Fijian Island of Taveuni the international date line cuts through the island giving you the chance to stand in two days at once. To the east of the line it is always one day ahead of the west of the line; you can be in the past and the present at the same time.

Step Back in Time

- The best time to visit is when there is a special event like Christmas – you can celebrate it twice – or a birthday, so you can stay younger for an extra day

Why have the line?
If the line didn't exist, anyone travelling westward would see the same day twice, anyone travelling eastward would be missing a day.

Stand on the International Date Line **Form**

Once you have completed this **Thing To Do**,
stick your Achieved Star here and fill in the form

Achieved

Place an X where you stood on the International Date Line

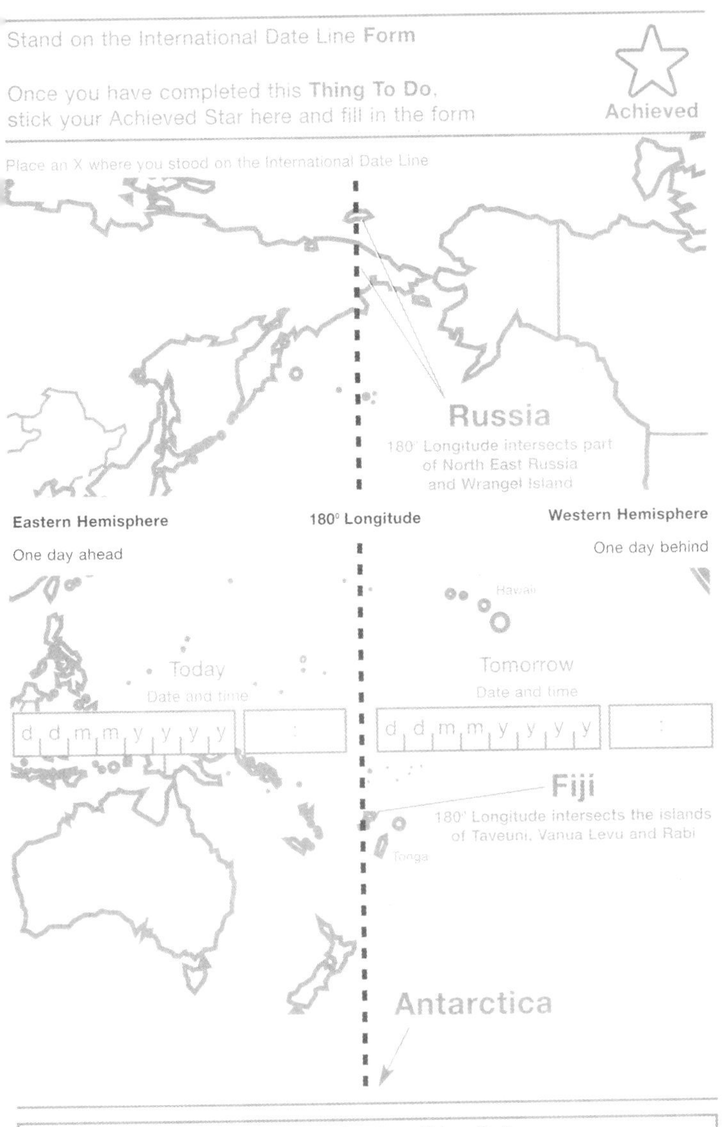

At the same time you could complete these **Things To Do**
36: Visit Every Country • 40: Get a Free Upgrade on a Plane •
62: Join the Mile High Club • 67: Visit ...

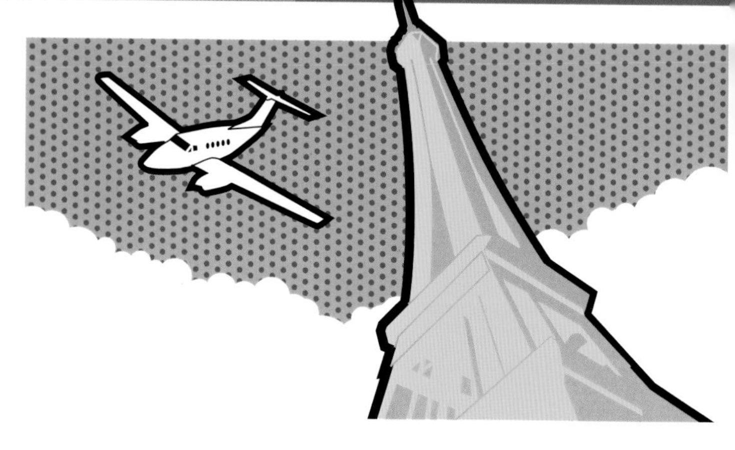

Learn to Fly a Plane

'No flying machine will ever fly from New York to Paris'

How wrong was Orville Wright? He may have been the first person ever to fly, on 17 December 1903, but within twenty-five years of his first flight, on 21 May 1927, Charles A. Lindbergh completed the first solo non-stop transatlantic flight from New York to Paris, in 33.5 hours.

Why put your life in someone else's hands when you fly? Take control, find inspiration from past accomplishments and learn to fly; this way you can cruise down to Paris and avoid queues, delays, cramped quarters and air rage.

Come Fly With Me

- The basic private pilot's licence allows you to fly a single-engine plane in weather with good visibility. You can take passengers but can't be paid for it
- To pass you'll need a medical examination, a good knowledge of English, to be at least 17 years old, a minimum of 32 hours flight experience and a written test
- It will cost around £3,500 ($6,600), and there may be extra fees such as plane rental, landing fees, etc

The first non-stop transatlantic flight was accomplished on 15 June 1919 – it took 16.5 hours – by John Alcock and Albert Brown from St John's in Newfoundland to Clifden in Ireland. Within the same month a prize of $25,000 was offered to the first person to fly from New York to Paris.

Get a Tattoo and/or a Piercing **Form**

Once you have completed this **Thing To Do**,
stick your Achieved Star here and fill in the form

Draw your tattoo(s) and piercing(s) in the correct position below

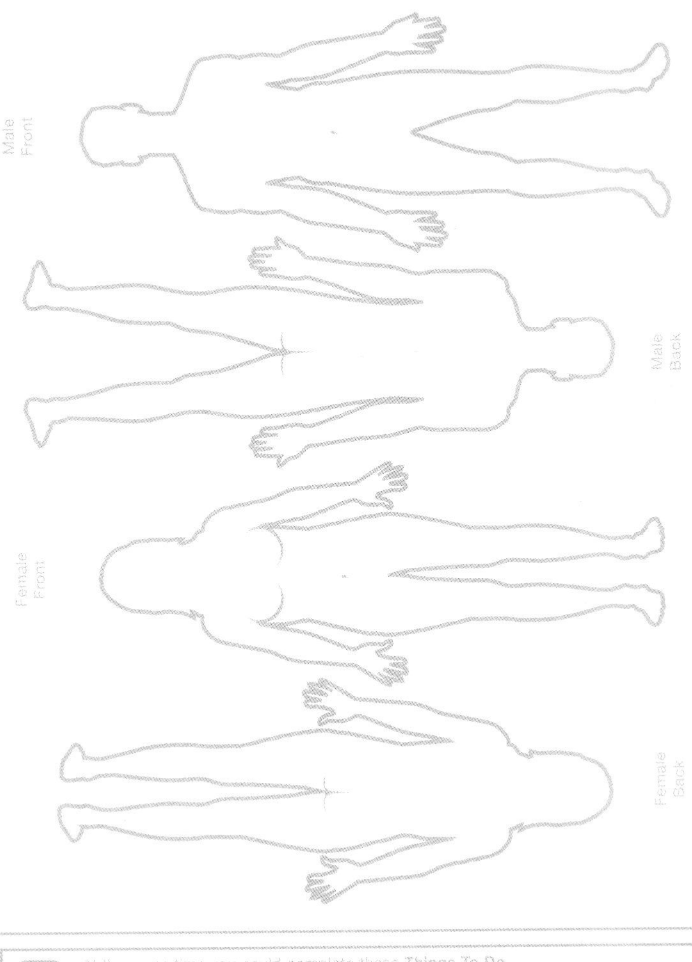

At the same time you could complete these **Things To Do**
16: Get into the *Guinness Book of World Records* *
17: Own a Pointless Collection

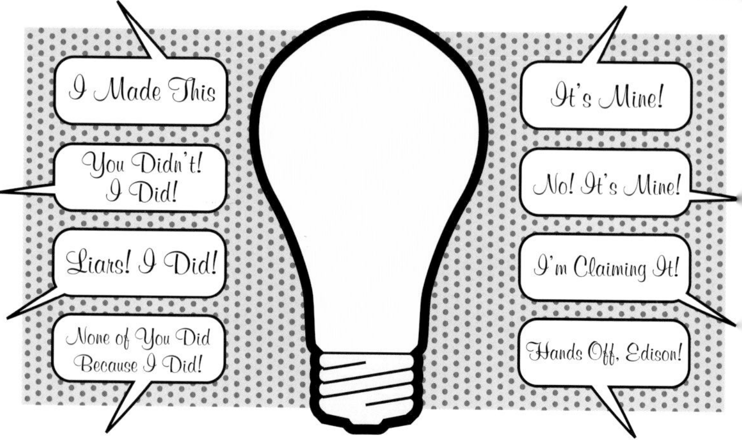

Invent Something

Every day we take hundreds of devices and items for granted, because they work perfectly and they make our lives much easier. It's when something doesn't work properly that swearing and threats of throwing it out of the window take over. It's time to find a replacement, but what if there isn't an alternative? You need to invent something that does exactly what it's supposed to do. Lock yourself in your shed and lose yourself in developing your invention, but be prepared to lose your temper, weeks of your time, money, friends and family as well.

One Vision

- As soon as you think of your idea, patent it so no one else can claim it as theirs
- Give your invention a grand-sounding name like the **Convotron** or the **Illumonac**
- Persevere; if it doesn't work, keep trying until it does

Who Invented the Light Bulb?

Well it wasn't **Thomas Edison**. 70 years before **Edison** in 1806 **Humphry Davy** demonstrated an electric lamp with a current passed through a strip. 1820: **Warren De La Rue** invented an incandescent lamp with a coil in a glass tube. 1835: **James Bowman Lindsay** demonstrated a constant electric light. 1840: **Sir William Grove**, illuminated a theatre with electric lamps. 1841: **Frederick De Moleyns** got the first patent for a bulb. 1845: **J.W. Starr** patented a bulb using a vacuum. 1854: Heinrich Göbel developed the first practical light bulb. 1875: **Woodward & Evan's** sold their bulb patent to **Thomas Edison**. 1878: an English physicist, **Joseph Swan**, patented a carbon filament lightbulb, a year later in 1879 Edison patented the same lightbulb. **Swan** successfully sued **Edison** and gained half of his company. They formed the Edison & Swan United Electric Light Company. So who invented the lightbulb? Your guess is as good as mine.

Great Inventions The wheel, the Archimedean screw, gunpowder, clocks, the battery, the bicycle, film and photography, television, the automobile, aeroplanes, the bra, condoms, tin cans, can openers, ballpoint pens, credit cards, computers, the internet.

Invent Something **Form**

Once you have completed this **Thing To Do**, stick your Achieved Star here and fill in the form

Achieved

Date and time you thought of your invention

d d m m y y y y :

How long did your idea take to develop?

Years Months Days

What is the name of your invention?

Have you had sponsorship from a company?

What is your invention designed to do?

How has it helped humanity?

Have you smashed it up because it wouldn't work? y/n

Has your idea been taken on by a company? y/n If yes, which one?

Approximately, how much did you spend developing your idea? THINGS TO DO £/$

How much did you get paid for the rights to your invention? THINGS TO DO £/$

Draw a blueprint for your invention below

At the same time you could complete these **Things To Do**

72: Have Enough Money to Do All the Things on This List •
94: Get Something Named After You

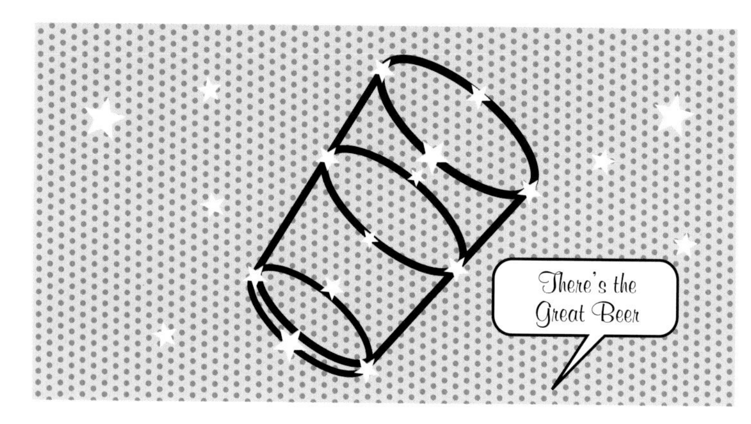

Learn Astronomy and Read the Night Sky

There are a lot more constellations in the night sky besides Orion and the Plough* (the only ones everyone seems to be able to identify). There are 88 constellations in all, the majority of which are based on characters from Greek mythology, although the constellations don't look like anything you can identify with ...

It's a huge task to identify all the constellations so here are a few of the better known ones for you to master, but the main challenge is to learn them and identify them without the aid of this book; when you've done so, you can tick the boxes.

The planets are harder to track but with the help of the **heavens-above.com** website, as well as the planets, you can also track the space shuttle when it's in orbit, the international space station and other satellites that orbit the Earth.

Distance from Sun (in miles)
Mercury 36 million miles
Venus 67 million miles
Earth 93 million miles
Mars 141 million miles
Jupiter 482 million miles
Saturn 886 million miles
Uranus 1.78 billion miles
Neptune 2.79 billion miles
Pluto 3.67 billion miles
Nearest star (Proxima Centauri) 25 trillion miles

***The Plough**
Technically the Plough isn't a constellation, it is part of the constellation know as Ursa Major or The Great Bear, but the plough shape is generally easily identified.

Learn Astronomy and Read the Night Sky Form
Once you have completed this Thing To Do,
stick your Achieved Star here and fill in the form
Achieved
Below is an area of the constellations in the northern hemisphere.
Tick box when successfully identified the constellation without the use of this book
Pegasus
Square of Pegasus
Cassiopeia
Cygnus
Cepheus
Perseus
Lyra
Ursa Minor
Polaris
Auriga
Draco
Gemini
Hercules
The Plough
Ursa Major
Cancer
Serpens Caput
Boötes
Leo
Have you seen these planets?
Mercury
Venus
Mars
Jupiter
Saturn
Uranus
Neptune
Pluto
At the same time you could complete these Things To Do
25: Capture the Moment in an Award-winning Photograph • 49: See Both Solar and Lunar Eclipses • 32: See the Aurora Borealis • 90: Join the 16-Mile High Club

Drink a Vintage Wine

What makes a vintage wine vintage?

A vintage wine is wine with a date on it; this is the year the grapes were harvested. Some fine wines can take many years to fully mature. But beware – a vintage can be bad as well as good.

What makes a good vintage?

Some wines (usually port) are only 'declared' in good years. What makes a good vintage wine is the quality of the fruit that particular year. This is primarily reliant on the weather being as perfect as possible throughout the growing season. When this happens, the winemakers of that region (such as Burgundy or Bordeaux) will declare it a 'good vintage'. But this can also be a marketing tool to increase sales so in fact it's the *great* vintages that you really have to look for.

Tips

- Make sure you're not the one paying
- Bluff your way through a wine conversation. Talk about colour, aroma and bouquet at great length and use the words 'structure', 'nose', 'body' and 'finesse' enthusiastically. You can also get a lot of mileage out of the word 'yes' when discussing wine
- Wine-tasting – swallow instead of spitting. Why waste good wine?

Expensive Taste
The Château d'Yquem Sauternes wine of 1787, from the Bordeaux region of France, is the most expensive wine in the world. It costs between $56,000 and $64,000 per bottle.

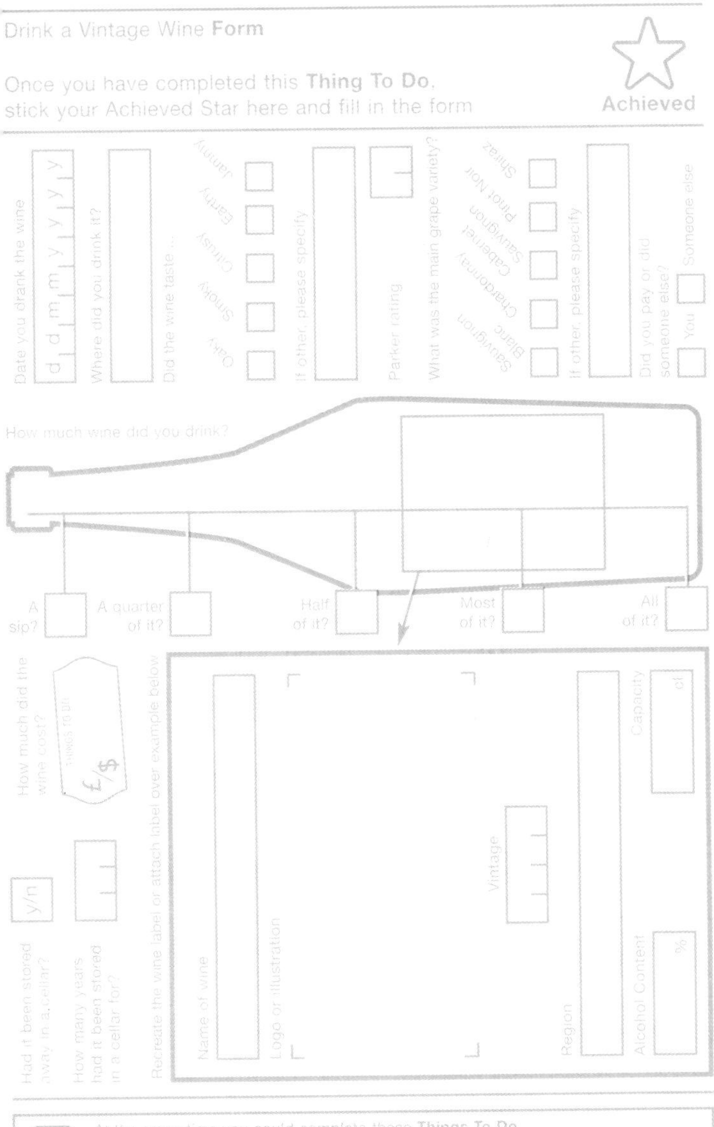

Drink a Vintage Wine Form
Once you have completed this Thing To Do, stick your Achieved Star here and fill in the form
Achieved
Date you drank the wine
d d m m y y y y
Where did you drink it?
Did the wine taste ...
Jammy
Earthy
Citrusy
Smoky
Oaky
If other, please specify
Parker rating
What was the main grape variety?
Shiraz
Pinot Noir
Cabernet Sauvignon
Chardonnay
Sauvignon Blanc
If other, please specify
Did you pay or did someone else?
You
Someone else
How much wine did you drink?
A sip?
A quarter of it?
Half of it?
Most of it?
All of it?
How much did the wine cost?
£/$
Had it been stored away in a cellar?
y/n
How many years had it been stored in a cellar for?
Recreate the wine label or attach label over example below
Name of wine
Logo or illustration
Vintage
Region
Capacity
cl
Alcohol Content
%

At the same time you could complete these **Things To Do**
65: Shout 'Drinks Are on Me!' in a Pub or a Bar • 72: Have Enough Money to Do All the Things on This List • 93: Complete the Monopoly Board Pub Crawl

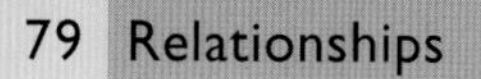

Answer a Personal Ad

You're casually flicking through the paper, nothing is catching your eye, it's just death, disaster and misery. Nothing holds your interest until you turn the page over and there are the personal ads. Bingo! You spend the next 20 minutes looking through ads such as:

Sampson seeks Delilah
Blonde, Tall, 35, Good Physique, No Hairdressers.

Why not answer one? You've spent enough time looking through them.

Anatomy of a Personal Ad

- Look for the amusing titles – 'Blair seeks Bush', 'Doctor to mend broken heart', 'Builder needs cement to plug hole'
- Key words – Slim, Curvy, Attractive, Passionate, Fun, Beautiful
- Understand acronyms such as GSOH (Good Sense of Humour), WLTM (Would Like To Meet), TLC (Tender Loving Care), LTR (Long Term Relationship), NTW (No Time Wasters)
- Avoid ads like this:

Tall, Dark
Skinny, boring, depressed, poor, happy failure, 35, seeks lonely woman for staying in.

Speed Date A way of meeting up to 30 potential dates in the same evening. Spend 3 minutes with each date, fill in a dating card and hand it in at the end of the evening; if you specify a person you'd like to meet and they specify you, the organiser will put you in touch.

Answer a personal Ad **Form**

Once you have completed this **Thing To Do**, stick your Achieved Star here and fill in the form

Achieved

Attach the ad or write in the space provided the details of the personal ad you answered

Where did you see the ad?

YOUR REPLY TO THE AD

Date you sent a reply: d d m m y y y y

Did you tell the truth about yourself? y/n If no, write some of your lies below:

THE REPLY TO YOUR REPLY

Date you got an answer: d d m m y y y y

Was the response you received:

Positive? Negative? Neither?

CORRESPONDENCE

How much correspondence did it take until you went on your date?

THE DATE

Date and time of your date d d m m y y y y :

Where was your date?

Did you see your date and walk straight back out the door? y/n

If yes, what was the reason for leaving?

What did the date involve?

A Meal | Drinks | Cinema | A Concert | A Museum | Other

THE BILL

Did you pay? Did they pay? Did you split it?

DATE ANALYSIS

Do you think the date went well? y/n Did you fancy your date? y/n

Do you feel you got on well? y/n Will you meet up again? y/n

THE AFTERMATH

Did you go back to their's for coffee? y/n Or was coffee at your's? y/n

Did the date result in a long term relationship?

y/n If yes, how long?

Is it still going? y/n Or is the relationship over now? y/n

At the same time you could complete these **Things To Do**
18: Study the *Kama Sutra* and Put Theory into Practice • 45: Do a Runner From a Fancy Restaurant • 71: Have Adventurous Sex • 78: Drink a Vintage Wine

Spend Christmas on the Beach

Parrots in your Christmas tree, tacky souvenirs in your crackers and sand in your Christmas pudding. The promise of a white Christmas usually ends in a snow no-show; if it's not overcast it's raining. If it's going to be snowless this Christmas, pack up your presents and head for the sun. Christmas is celebrated the world over although, in hot places, the traditional Christmas dinners are substituted for barbecues; in the Caribbean Christmas carols are played on steel drums; and in the southern hemisphere Christmas day lasts longer as it's only a few days behind the longest day on 21 December, compared to our shortest day in the northern hemisphere. Remember to pack the presents, your swimming costume and don't forget the sun cream.

Thank God It's Christmas

- Make a snowball from the ice in your freezer and catch an unsuspecting sun bather with it. Make sure you're on target as your freezer will only have enough 'snow' for one snowball
- If you live in Australia or somewhere hot, spend Christmas somewhere cold like England. Be prepared for the fact that England isn't like 19th century London in **A Christmas Carol** at Christmas

Merry Christmas! Afrikaans – **Geseënde Kersfees** • Hawaiian – **Mele Kalikimaka** • Spanish – **Feliz Navidad** • Greek – **Kala Christouyenna!** • Samoan – **Manuia Le Kirisimasi** • Estonian – **Ruumsaid Juuluplhi** • Finnish – **Hyvaa Joulua**

Spend Christmas on the Beach **Form**

Once you have completed this **Thing To Do**, stick your Achieved Star here and fill in the form

Achieved

Date and time you spent Christmas on the beach

2 5 1 2 :

Which country were you in?

Which beach were you on?

Which hemisphere were you in?

Northern Hemisphere

Southern Hemisphere

Which season was it?

Summer

Winter

What was the temperature on the beach? °C

Who did you spend Christmas on the beach with?

Family | Friends | Partner | Your Pets | Total Strangers | On Your Own

Did you ...

... sing Christmas Carols? y/n

... have fake snow? y/n

... play Christmas songs? y/n

... have crackers and hats? y/n

... play Christmas party games? y/n

... wear a santa outfit or hat? y/n

... have a traditional Christmas dinner? y/n

... decorate a palm tree? y/n

Or did you bring your own tree? y/n

Place a photograph of your Christmas on the beach

At the same time you could complete these **Things To Do**

36: Visit Every Country • 43: Throw a Dart into a Map and Travel to Where it Lands • 58: Live in the Place You Love • 78: Drink a Vintage Wine

Get Barred From a Pub or Bar

You've already made a load of new friends by giving them all free drinks (see **Thing To Do** No. 65); now it's time to make them pay for your generosity.

Choosing Your Pub

- Don't get barred from your local, this would be a foolish decision. Instead choose a pub or bar in a different town altogether. Try to get barred from one bar only, and not all the drinking dens in the region

How to Be Unpopular

- Upset the locals, a sure fire way to get barred
- Be too drunk to hold a pint
- Take over the games room from the kids
- Shout 'Drinks are on me!' and don't pay
- Expose yourself
- Turn up at a small pub or bar with fifty friends. Each person asks for a different cocktail, the more difficult to make, the better. Each person complains about their cocktail and demands a new one
- Go behind the bar and pour your own drinks

How Not to Get Barred
Own your own pub or bar; this is one way you'll never get thrown out. You've got the power. Who stays, who goes? Throw people out for the hell of it.

Get Barred From a Pub or Bar **Form**

Once you have completed this **Thing To Do**, stick your Achieved Star here and fill in the form

Draw the scene in the pub that resulted in you being barred

Detail the incident ...

Date and time you were barred

d d m m y y y y :

What was the name of the pub/bar?

Where was the pub/bar?

Were you a regular before the incident? y/n

If no, why were you there?

Did your friends get thrown out as well as you? y/n

Which of the following statements are true. Tick the corresponding box

	True	False
It was a case of mistaken identity		
I deserved it		
I have never been allowed back since		
I was barred from all the pubs and bars in the region as well		
I was allowed back after the management changed		
I wouldn't go back even if you paid me		

At the same time you could complete these **Things To Do**
10: Leave Your Mark in Graffiti • 23: Get Arrested • 65: Shout 'Drinks Are on Me!' in a Pub or a Bar • 60: Take Part in a Police Line-up

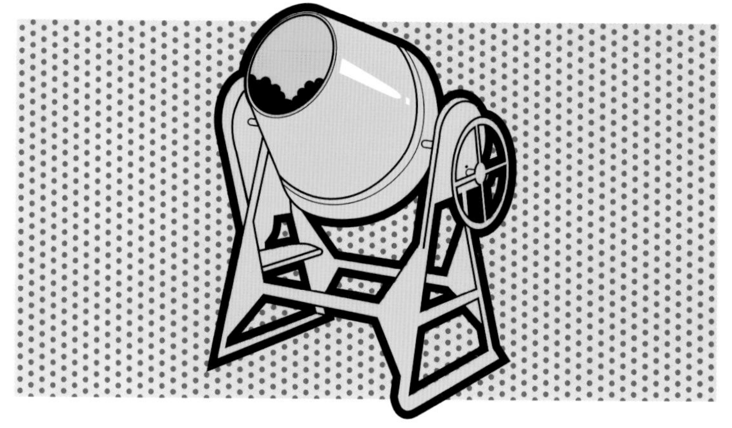

Build Your Own House

For some people, owning their own house is a dream come true, but for others this isn't enough. Imagine living in a house that you've designed, built and considered every detail for. Create something truly individual: turn a disused factory into a four floor minimalist showhome, turn a rundown church into a cosy retreat or start from scratch and build a house made out of straw or a mock Tudor castle with far too many turrets. Whatever you decide to build, there are a few things to consider that might just put you off ...

Things to Consider ...

- It will take years to build, from original concept to finished building
- As the build starts, you'll have to juggle working to pay the bills, visiting the site, keeping the builders happy and keeping a lid on all your partner's extravagant demands
- You'll go over budget and you'll miss all your deadlines
- You'll need an understanding bank manager (he'll come in handy when the costs start to spiral out of control)
- Be prepared to feel every emotion possible and perhaps discover some new ones

Still up for it? Well, the quicker you start planning the sooner you can be the envy of your friends with your ultimate party showhome.

Do Not Attempt Without Competent Supervision: anything to do with the electric, gas or water supply, the installation of specialist equipment or anything that needs measurements to the exact millimetre. You don't want to destroy everything you've just built.

Build Your Own House **Form**

Once you have completed this **Thing To Do**, stick your Achieved Star here and fill in the form

Achieved

When did you start the build? d d m m y y y y

When were you due to move in? d d m m y y y y

When did you actually move in? d d m m y y y y

How long did the project take?

Years Months Weeks

What do you have inside your house? How many ...

Bedrooms do you have?

Toilets do you have?

Bathrooms do you have?

Gardens do you have?

Living areas do you have?

Kitchens do you have?

Do you have?

A swimming pool?

A bar?

An office?

A games room?

A patio?

A Jacuzzi?

A roof terrace?

A double garage?

A walk-in fridge freezer?

A gym?

A huge garden?

A fountain?

Would you do it again? y/n

Have you had your house valued? y/n

How much has your house been valued at? £/$

FINAL INVOICE

Cost of land £/$

Labour costs £/$

Building costs £/$

Materials £/$

Other costs £/$

Equipment hire costs £/$

TOTAL PROJECT COST

£/$

What had you estimated the final cost to be? £/$

At the same time you could complete these **Things To Do**

58: Live in the Place You Love • 72: Have Enough Money to Do All the Things on This List

Skinny Dip at Midnight

Throw caution and your clothes to the wind. Skinny dipping is illegal in most places around the world but don't let that stop you. Get drunk, get them off and try not to get caught with your pants down.

I Want to Break Free

- Pick somewhere with a warm climate for skinny dipping in the sea
- Be aware of the dangers. Keep a look-out for sharks at night, they'll see you well before you see them. Remember what happened to the girl at the start of **Jaws**? Keep an eye out for jellyfish and other dangerous creatures
- Don't choose a nudist beach as you'll be hanging around with a big bunch of middle-aged naked people who do this for a living
- Skinny dipping inland: head for secluded waterfalls and rivers and hot springs
- Make sure you're not with any pranksters who are going to steal your clothes as soon as you're in the water. If you are, make sure one of them is you
- Don't get arrested for indecent exposure

Warning! The Candiru fish in the Amazon is known to swim up urine streams and into your bladder, causing excruciating pain. It is 50mm (2in) long and 5mm (1/4in) wide and has extendable spines. Only surgery can remove it. Be careful, don't drip while you dip.

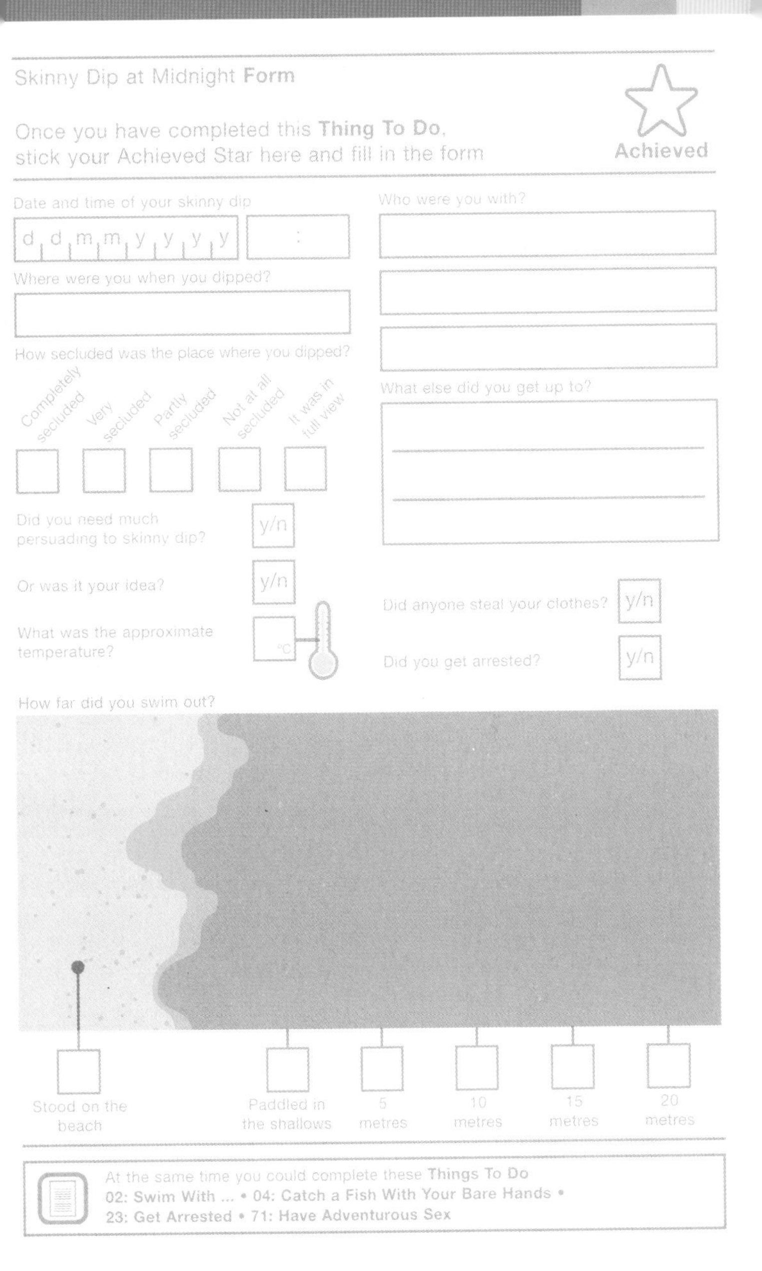

Skinny Dip at Midnight **Form**

Once you have completed this **Thing To Do**, stick your Achieved Star here and fill in the form

Achieved

Date and time of your skinny dip

d d m m y y y y :

Where were you when you dipped?

How secluded was the place where you dipped?

Completely secluded | Very secluded | Partly secluded | Not at all secluded | It was in full view

Did you need much persuading to skinny dip? y/n

Or was it your idea? y/n

What was the approximate temperature? °C

Who were you with?

What else did you get up to?

Did anyone steal your clothes? y/n

Did you get arrested? y/n

How far did you swim out?

Stood on the beach | Paddled in the shallows | 5 metres | 10 metres | 15 metres | 20 metres

At the same time you could complete these **Things To Do**
02: Swim With ... • 04: Catch a Fish With Your Bare Hands • 23: Get Arrested • 71: Have Adventurous Sex

Sell all Your Junk on eBay and Make a Profit

Bucket of water

Never been used, highest bidder wins, must collect*

You can sell pretty much anything on eBay. No matter how ridiculous it seems, there is always someone out there willing to buy your junk. Clear out your garage, get rid of the one ski you've been hanging on to, sell the unwanted Christmas presents. Try to sell any unsaleable items too, like a can of paint with a brush stuck in it, paint gone hard, highest bidder wins, just don't re-spend the money you've made on eBay back on eBay or you'll end up with more junk than you started with, and you'll clean out your garage only to discover that you've filled the spare room.

Buying

- Before you bid, check the high-street price; some people don't check and end up paying more for no reason
- Don't think you've won until you've been told you've won; there are people out there who bid at the last second

Selling

- Put everything up for sale – someone, somewhere will buy it eventually
- Set up an eBay shop – indulge all your spare time on eBay. Sell things abroad that you can only get over here and make a fortune

***Bucket of Water Sale** A bucket of 'fabulous Bristol tap water' was sold for £255 on eBay in the UK in October 2003. Usually these kinds of 'joke' auctions are shut down immediately but it was kept open as all the proceeds went to charity.

Sell All Your Junk and Make a Profit **Form**

Once you have completed this **Thing To Do**, stick your Achieved Star here and fill in the form

Achieved

Date and time

d d m m y y y y :

What was your auction name? What was the total feedback number you gained? Write the number in the brackets and colour the star to the corresponding colour you gained

(☆)

How many items did you attempt to sell?

How many items actually sold?

What was the daftest item you posted on eBay?

Did it sell? y/n If yes, how much? THINGS TO DO £/$

Which item went for the most money?

How much did it make? THINGS TO DO £/$

Which items didn't sell?

Did you try and resell or did you keep them?

Keep them y/n Tried to resell them y/n

Were there some items you couldn't bring yourself to sell?If there were, list them below

Feedback

How many of your responses were ...

Positive Neutral Negative

What was your overall percentage of positive feedback? %

What was your best comment?

And the worst?

What was your grand total? THINGS TO DO £/$

Buying

Did you end up buying things as well as selling? y/n

How much did you spend on eBay? THINGS TO DO £/$

At the same time you could complete these **Things To Do**

17: Own a Pointless Collection • 72: Have Enough Money to Do All the Things on This List

Visit the World's Tallest Buildings

By the time you get around to completing this **Thing To Do** there will probably be even taller buildings built since you started visiting the ones on the list.

The world's tallest buildings list is often disputed. Do you measure up to the top of the building or to the tip of the antenna on the roof of the building?

This list features the buildings measured up to the top of the spires, which makes the tallest building **Taipei 101** in Taiwan (without the spire the world's tallest building would be the Petronas Towers in Kuala Lumpa, Malaysia). Not only that, there are other structures that are even taller than these buildings; the world's tallest structure is the CN Tower in Toronto which stands at a height of 1,815ft.

Confusing? Keep the correction fluid handy.

World's Tallest Towers

Canadian National Tower, Toronto, Canada (1,815ft)

Ostankino Tower, Moscow, Russia (1,762ft)

Oriental Pearl Tower, Shanghai, China (1,535ft)

Menara Kuala Lumpur, Malaysia (1,403ft)

Central Radio & TV Tower, Beijing, China (1,369ft)

Tianjin TV Tower, Tianjin, China (1,362ft)

LORAN-C Tower, Port Clarence, Alaska, (1,350ft)

Tashkent Tower, Tashkent, Uzbekistan (1,230ft)

Liberation Tower, Kuwait City, Kuwait (1,214ft)

Fernsehturm Tower, Berlin, Germany (1,198ft)

The Difference Between Structures and Buildings
The CN Tower is considered a structure because it isn't habitable and it cannot be used for office space.

Visit the World's Tallest Buildings **Form**

Once you have completed this **Thing To Do**, stick your Achieved Star here and fill in the form

Below are the ten tallest buildings in the world at present, (white) and buildings that are either proposed or currently under construction (grey). There are many other proposed buildings, these are a few of the most likely ones to be completed

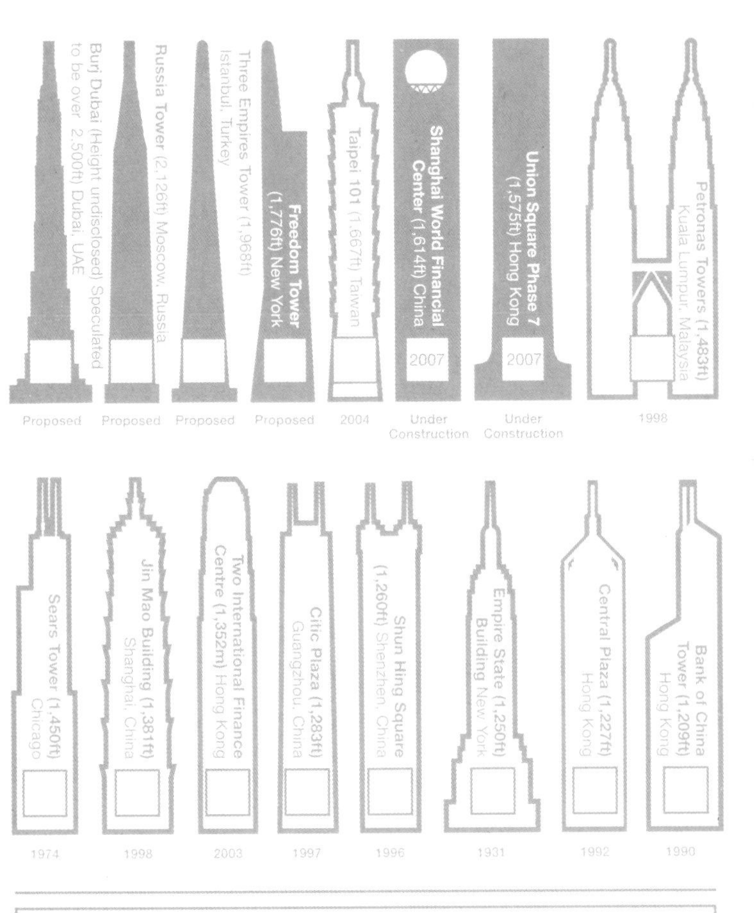

At the same time you could complete these **Things To Do**
25: Capture the Moment in an Award-winning Photograph • 88: Get Married Unusually • 71: Have Adventurous Sex

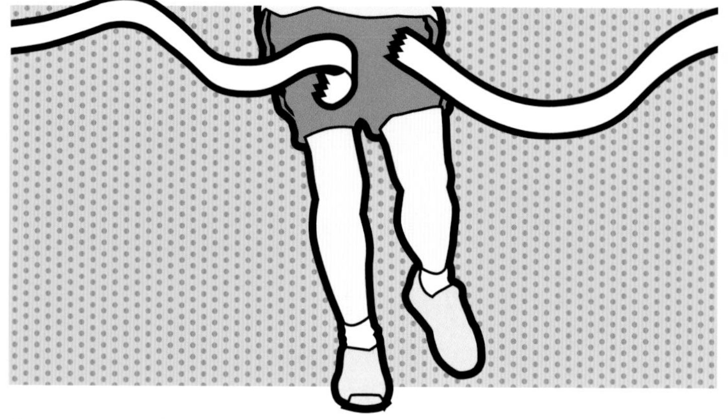

Run a Marathon

There are so many people wanting to do a marathon these days that it can be hours after the start gun has gone off before you even cross the start line; by then the fastest runners have finished before you've even got underway. But don't let that put you off, all you have to do is run 26.275 miles once you do eventually get going.

Before you set off, make sure you've got all the parts to your Spiderman costume. You don't want to embarrass yourself now, do you?

Make sure you choose a streamline costume. Don't choose an outfit that will slow you down like a full deep sea diving outfit. It'll take you a week to cross the start line.

Whatever you decide to wear, make sure you've remembered to bring your charity bucket and your 'Hello Mum' sign.

Marathon History In 490BC, during the Persian-Greek War, Phidippides, a professional runner, ran to Athens to inform the Athenians of the victory at Marathon, 26 miles away; he died of exhaustion after delivering the message.

Run a Marathon **Form**

Once you have completed this **Thing To Do**, stick your Achieved Star here and fill in the form

Achieved

Date and race start time

d d m m y y y y :

Which marathon did you run?

Start time :

Finish time :

Did you finish the course? y/n

If yes, what position did you finish in?

How many attempts at a marathon did it take before you finally finished one?

How long did the marathon take you to run?

Weeks | Days | Hours | Minutes | Seconds

Did you get onto TV? y/n

Did you get interviewed? y/n

Did you get cramp? y/n

How many blisters did you get?

Did you get a medal for finishing the course? y/n

Did you run for charity? y/n

If yes, how much did you raise? £/$

Which charity did you raise the money for?

Did you do enough training before the marathon? y/n

How many hours a week did you train? hrs

Did you dress in a costume? y/n

Draw your costume below

Write your number in here

Would you run a marathon again?

Yes | Maybe | I'd have to think hard about it | Never again | Never EVER again

At the same time you could complete these **Things To Do**

03: Win an Award, Trophy or Prize • 16: Get into the *Guinness Book of World Records* • 88: Get Married Unusually

Conquer Your Fear

Fear is a hindrance. Irrational fears take up too much unwanted pain and anguish. So why not face your fear head on? If it's heights, bungee jump (see **Thing To Do** No. 26), if you're scared of the dark (also known as achluophobia) learn to sleep with the light off ... or try the rational approach and face your phobia that way. Take flying for example – the odds of dying in a plane crash are 1 in 1.5 million. There are twice as many deaths on the road in one year than in aircraft accidents since air travel began and compare this to the odds of dying in your bathtub which are 1 in 10,455. You do the math – and book yourself on the next flight to Timbuktu.

It might take you your whole life to overcome your darkest fear and complete this **Thing To Do** and even then, you might not conquer it, all you can do is give it a try; if that doesn't work, try hypnotism.

Top Ten Fears

1. ARACHNOPHOBIA
Fear of spiders
2. SOCIOPHOBIA
Fear of people or social situations
3. AVIATOPHOBIA
Fear of flying
4. AGORAPHOBIA
Fear of open spaces
5. CLAUSTROPHOBIA
Fear of confined spaces
6. EMETOPHOBIA
Fear of vomiting
7. ACROPHOBIA
Fear of heights
8. CANCERPHOBIA
Fear of cancer
9. BRONTOPHOBIA
Fear of thunder and lightning
10. NECROPHOBIA
Fear of death

Other Phobias: Ecclesiophobia: Fear of church, Dishabillophobia: Fear of undressing in front of someone, Hippopotomonstrosesquippedaliophobia: Fear of long words, Cybergphobia: Fear of computers, Panphobia: Fear of anything and everything

Conquer Your Fear **Form**

Once you have completed this **Thing To Do**, stick your Achieved Star here and fill in the form

How did your fear originate?

What is your fear?

Date you tackled your fear: d d m m y y y y

Write your fear diary here

How many years had it affected you?

Did you need therapy? y/n

Did you conquer your fear? y/n

Do you still have nightmares? y/n

At the same time you could complete these **Things To Do**

26: Bungee Jump • 28: Sky Dive • 46: Scuba Dive • 74: Learn to Fly a Plane

Get Married Unusually

In Space, Naked, Underwater, as Elvis, On Motorbikes ... Getting married is all about getting what you want out of your big day. You can try to get married anywhere as long as you can persuade the vicar/official to do whatever you want to do. Remember, it's your day, not your mother-in-law's.

Wedding Ideas

- Get married at 30,000ft. The plane would take off for your honeymoon destination. The ceremony would be performed mid flight in first class by the captain and be played on the in-flight video screens for the rest of the guests. After the ceremony, there is dancing in the aisles, The only downside is that the whole wedding party would be joining you on your honeymoon
- While hang-gliding
- Take part in the world's biggest ever joint wedding ceremony
- A fancy dress movie-themed wedding. You could have a wedding based on the **Wizard of Oz,** the guest dress code could be Munchkins and Flying Monkeys. The mother-in-law can be the Wicked Witch
- Fake your own wedding. This way you get all the reward without any of the red tape

'I Do ... No I Don't'
Get married in Las Vegas drunk as a skunk and have it annulled within 24 hours – see the marriage of Britney Spears marriage to childhood friend Jason Allen Alexander.

Get Married Unusually **Form**

Once you have completed this **Thing To Do**, stick your Achieved Star here and fill in the form

Achieved

Date and time

d d m m y y y y

Who did you marry?

How did you get married unusually?

Where did the marriage take place?

Which religion did you get married under?

Did the mother-in-law take over? y/n

If yes, did you tell her where to go? y/n

Did your favourite band play at the wedding? y/n

If yes, which band was it?

Did anyone contest the wedding? y/n

If yes, who?

Draw in your unusual wedding scene, including guests, venue, outfits and other elements of your big day

Did something go wrong? If yes, list below

Are you still married? y/n

Would you do it again? y/n

At the same time you could complete these **Things To Do**

26: Bungee Jump • 31: Experience Weightlessness • 34: Design Your Own Cocktail • 72: Have Enough Money to Do All the Things on This List

It's Time You
Learned To Cook

Throw Away the Instant Noodles

Chop, peel, bake, grill, whip, whisk and sauté. There's more to cooking than quick cook pasta and TV dinners. It's one thing watching a cookery programme and another to attempt the meals in them. It's about time you mastered some new dishes to add to your weekly repertoire.

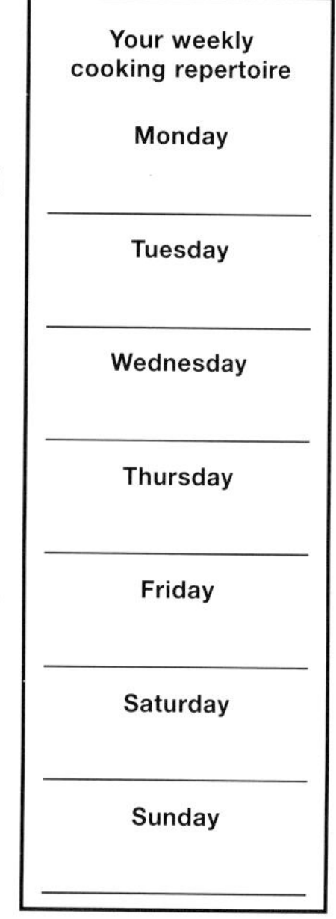

Your weekly cooking repertoire

Monday

Tuesday

Wednesday

Thursday

Friday

Saturday

Sunday

Cook Off

- Cook to impress. You can't go wrong with meals prepared for birthdays, anniversaries and Valentine's Day as long as you've had plenty of practice beforehand. Practice on flatmates and friends. They'll be thankful for a free experimental meal
- Don't get stuck in a food rut – cook yourself something different every night of the week
- Give yourself one takeaway night even if it is a kebab on Friday night on the way home from a drinking session

Rice Up Your Life
Rice is the world's most popular food. 76 million tonnes of rice is cultivated each year and it's the staple diet of over half the world's population.

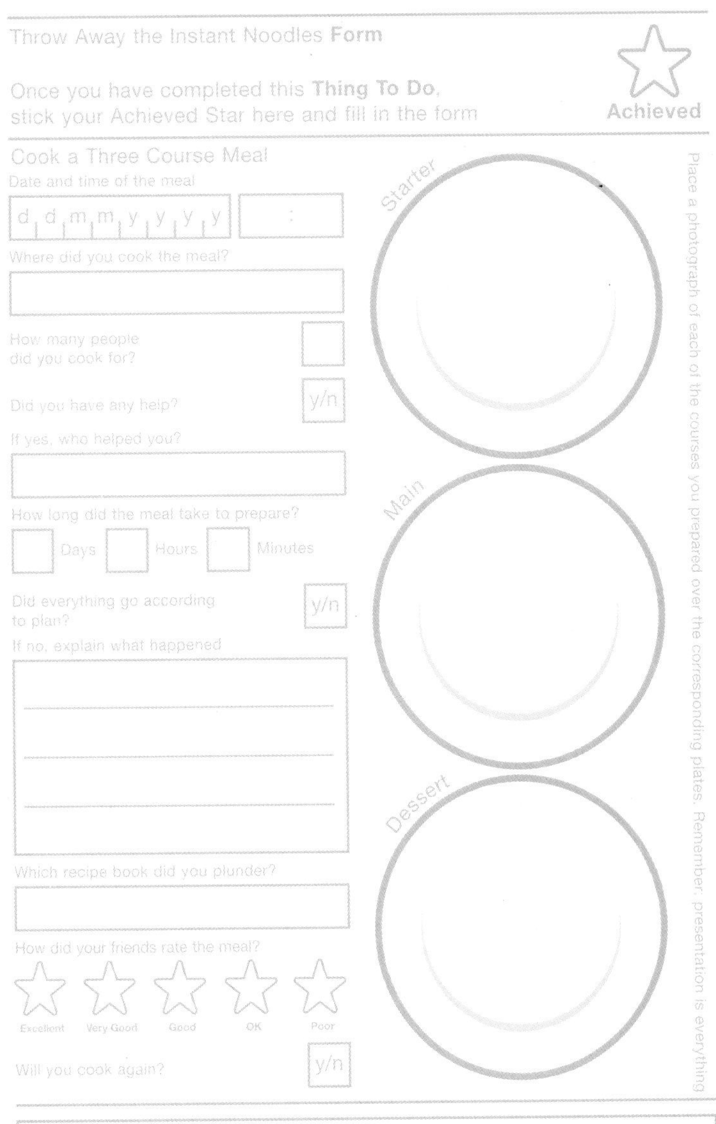

Throw Away the Instant Noodles **Form**

Once you have completed this **Thing To Do**, stick your Achieved Star here and fill in the form

Achieved

Cook a Three Course Meal

Date and time of the meal

d d m m y y y y :

Where did you cook the meal?

How many people did you cook for?

Did you have any help? y/n

If yes, who helped you?

How long did the meal take to prepare?

Days Hours Minutes

Did everything go according to plan? y/n

If no, explain what happened

Which recipe book did you plunder?

How did your friends rate the meal?

Excellent Very Good Good OK Poor

Will you cook again? y/n

Starter
Main
Dessert
Place a photograph of each of the courses you prepared over the corresponding plates. Remember: presentation is everything

At the same time you could complete these **Things To Do**
06: Throw a House Party When Your Parents Are Out • 34: Design Your Own Cocktail • 70: Invent a Word That Makes it into the Dictionary

Join the 16-Mile High Club

Rather than taking your clothes off to join the mile high club, you've got to put protective clothing on to join the 16-mile high club.

Since the passing of Concorde we've got to find other ways to fly supersonically. This can be achieved with a flight in the MiG-25 fighter jet. Concorde flew at twice the speed of sound, the MiG-25 can reach Mach 3. But there are other reasons to take part in this **Thing To Do**.

In half a hour you'll travel 16 miles (80,000ft) upwards to the edge of the atmosphere. Above you is nothing but blackness, below you you'll see the blue sky and you will also see the curvature of the Earth. At this point, the only other people higher than you are the astronauts on the International Space Station.

If you wanted to be an astronaut this is a more realistic way to see Earth from space as long as you've a plane ticket to Moscow, a little time to hand and $12,000. In some cases you can get a chance to fly it as well.

Concorde Facts Concorde could fly a mile in 2.5 seconds (23 miles a minute), it could outrun a rifle bullet by flying at Mach 2, (1,336mph, twice the speed of sound) and it flew at a height of 60,000ft (11 miles) above the earth. Concorde's final flight was on 24 October 2003.

Join the 16-Mile High Club **Form**

Once you have completed this **Thing To Do**, stick your Achieved Star here and fill in the form

Achieved

Mark on the diagram below the highest point you've travelled. Only fill in the star if you've travelled on Concorde, which flies at a height of 11 miles, or in a MiG-25, which travels at 16 miles

Ozone Layer

Highest balloon flight and highest sky dive record

MiG-25

16-Mile High Club

Concorde

11-Mile High Club

Everest

35,000ft Plane cruise height

Date you flew

d d m m y y y y

Which aircraft did you fly?

How fast did you fly? mph

How far did you fly? miles

How high did you fly? ft

How long was the journey? Hours Mins Secs

Where did you fly from?

... And where did you fly to?

Describe the experience

At the same time you could complete these **Things To Do**

16: Get into the *Guinness Book of World Records* • 31: Experience Weightlessness • 72: Have Enough Money to Do All the Things on This List • 74: Learn to Fly a Plane

Publish a Cult Website

The internet has changed everything; you can get anything you want delivered to your front door without having to talk to any moody shop assistants or leaving your house. The invention of the internet brought the mountain to Mohammad, it also brought him online shopping, gambling and porn. Everything you need, and everything you don't, is at your fingertips. So, if you want your ideas to be shared the world over, set up a cult website. Barricade yourself into your bedroom for weeks and work on your plans for world internet domination and untold riches ...

What the World is Waiting For

- Make it entertaining, pointless, funny and addictive. Your website should be designed to distract office workers from their work for hours on end
- Send a link for your site to ten people you know, and if your site is a hit, it'll be passed on, and on, and on ...
- Try to get your site's web address to the top search engines
- Do not use popups, they piss everyone off
- Offer a service and try and make money from it; once your site takes off, give up your day job (see **Thing To Do** No. 59) and expand

***Time* Magazine**
Every year *Time* **magazine** presents an award for 'Man of the Year'. In 1982 the Man of the Year was the computer.

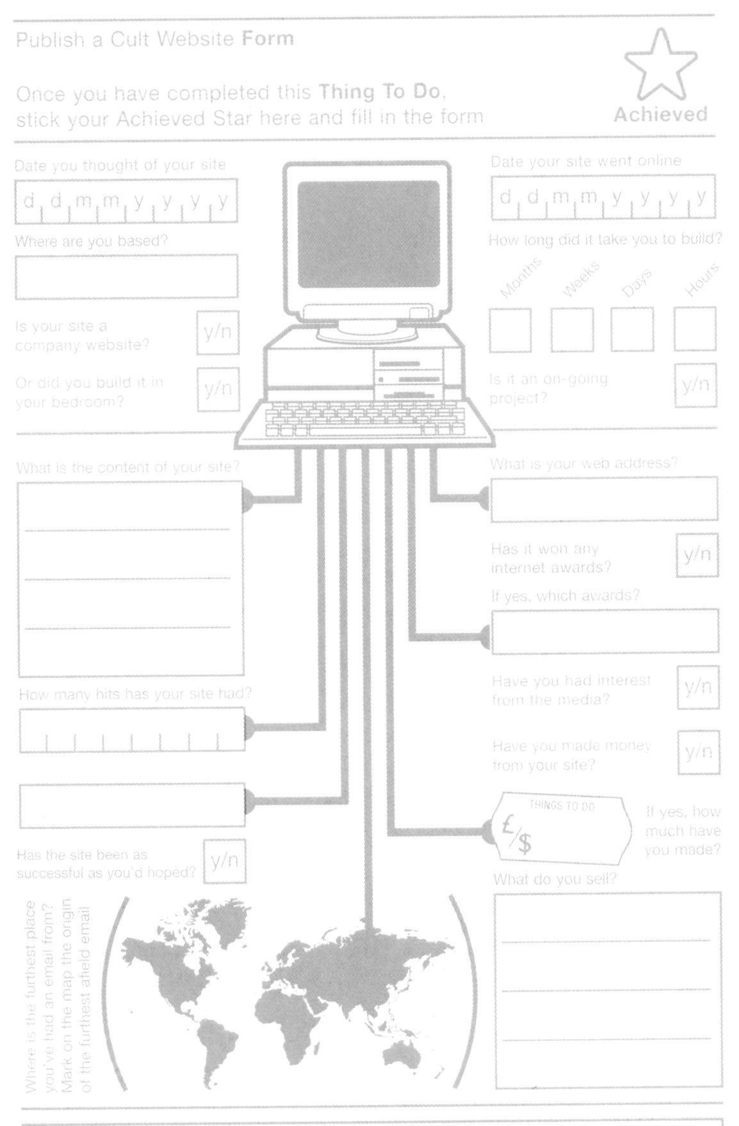

Publish a Cult Website **Form**

Once you have completed this **Thing To Do**, stick your Achieved Star here and fill in the form

Achieved

Date you thought of your site

d d m m y y y y

Where are you based?

Is your site a company website? y/n

Or did you build it in your bedroom? y/n

Date your site went online

d d m m y y y y

How long did it take you to build?

Months Weeks Days Hours

Is it an on-going project? y/n

What is the content of your site?

How many hits has your site had?

Has the site been as successful as you'd hoped? y/n

Where is the furthest place you've had an email from? Mark on the map the origin of the furthest afield email

What is your web address?

Has it won any internet awards? y/n

If yes, which awards?

Have you had interest from the media? y/n

Have you made money from your site? y/n

THINGS TO DO £/$

If yes, how much have you made?

What do you sell?

At the same time you could complete these **Things To Do**

16: Get into the *Guinness Book of World Records* • 72: Have Enough Money to Do All the Things on This List • 95: Get Revenge

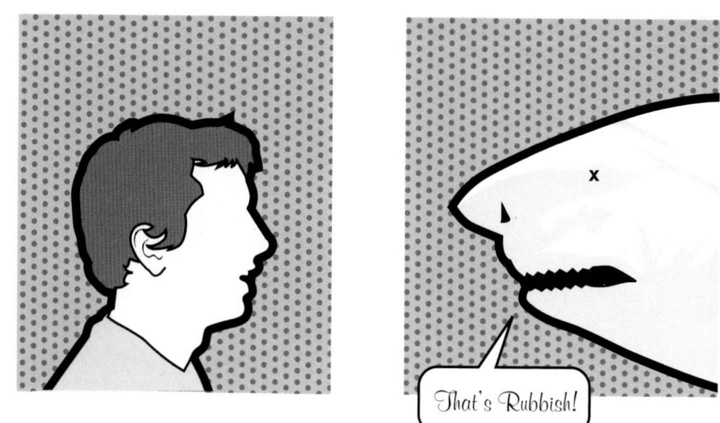

Own an Original Work of Art

Art can be split into two categories, 'Love' and 'Hate'. For instance, a 14ft shark in a tank of formaldehyde might be a work of genius to some people, but to many it's exactly what it is, a 14ft shark in a tank. Some people are prepared to pay millions for it, others wouldn't pay a cent for it. At the end of the day art is a matter of individual taste.

Choosing Your Artwork

Unless you've got millions in the bank to burn, choose your artwork carefully. You don't want to get bored of your choice a year after forking out thousands of pounds for it; if you have got millions in the bank, and you have got bored with your art, think of it as an investment.

Comments You May Encounter

- 'I know nothing about art but I know what I like'
- 'Where can I get one?'
- 'What the hell is that?'
- 'How much!?!'

Expensive Art Sales *Portrait of Dr Gachet* by Van Gogh sold for **$82.5m**. *Moulin de la Galette, 1876* by Renoir sold for **$78.1m**. *Self-portrait without beard* by Van Gogh sold for **$71.5m**. *Still Life With Curtain, Pitcher, and Bowl of Fruit* by Cezanne sold for **$60.5m**. *The Dream* by Picasso sold for **$48.4m**. *Sunday Afternoon on the Island of La Grane Jatte* by Seurat sold for **$35.2m**.

Own an Original Work of Art **Form**

Once you have completed this **Thing To Do**, stick your Achieved Star here and fill in the form

Achieved

Date of Purchase

d d m m y y y y

How old is it?

yrs

Which category does the work fall into?

Painting | Portrait | Drawing | Sculpture | Photograph | Print

Who is it by?

How long did it take for you to decide to buy it?

Months | Weeks | Days | Hours | Minutes | Seconds

Furniture & fittings | Jewellery | Ceramics | Building | Artwork commission | Other

Why did you buy it?

Loved it | For the collection | Investment | You know the artist | Other

How much did it cost?

THINGS TO DO £/$

... And, how much is it worth?

THINGS TO DO £/$

Where did you acquire it from?

Would you consider selling it?

y/n If yes how much would it take? £

Artwork details. Fill in the card, cut it out and place next to your work of art

Title

Year

Artist Name

Size

Materials Used

Description of Work

At the same time you could complete these **Things To Do**

17: Own a Pointless Collection • 63: Make the Front Page of a National Newspaper • 54: Make at Least One Huge Purchase You Can't Afford

Complete the Monopoly Board Pub Crawl (London)

Play the Game / Objective

Drink your way around the Monopoly board in one day by visiting a bar at all of the roads and stations mentioned in the game. Consume a drink in each.

Route

Choose the shortest route between venues. Visit a pub at each of the 22 streets and 4 stations on the board. Try and start with Old Kent Road and end in Mayfair.

What You Need

- An *A to Z* and a prepared route
- Photocopy the form 13 times, keep a record of each destination, once completed, attached the extra pages to the form opposite
- Enough money to pay for at least 26 drinks, food and travel (Buy a one day travel pass)
- A strong stomach

Tick off once visited

- ☐ Old Kent Rd
- ☐ Whitechapel Rd
- ☐ Marylebone Stn
- ☐ Euston Rd
- ☐ Pentonville Rd
- ☐ Angel, Islington
- ☐ Pall Mall
- ☐ Whitehall
- ☐ Northumberland Ave
- ☐ Liverpool St Stn
- ☐ Bow St
- ☐ Marlborough St
- ☐ Vine St
- ☐ Fleet St
- ☐ Strand
- ☐ Trafalgar Sq
- ☐ King's Cross Stn
- ☐ Coventry St
- ☐ Piccadilly
- ☐ Leicester Sq
- ☐ Oxford St
- ☐ Regent St
- ☐ Bond St
- ☐ Fenchurch St
- ☐ Park Lane
- ☐ Mayfair

Other Monopoly Board Pub Crawls to Attempt
Birmingham, Brazil, Canada, Edinburgh, the European Union, Hawaii, Hollywood, Hong Kong, Japan, Las Vegas, Paris, Reading, Russia and Zurich

Complete the Monopoly Board Pub Crawl **Form**

Once you have completed this **Thing To Do**, stick your Achieved Star here and fill in the form

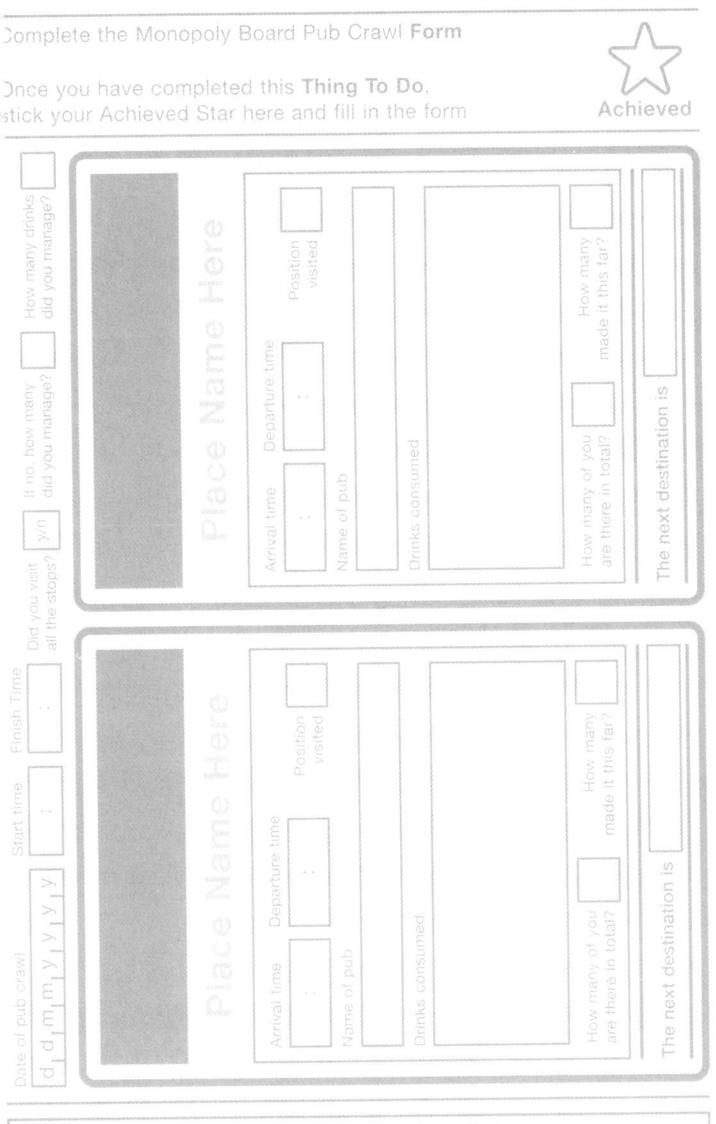
Achieved

Date of pub crawl d d m m y y y y

Start time :

Finish Time :

Did you visit all the stops? y/n

If no, how many did you manage?

How many drinks did you manage?

Place Name Here

Arrival time :

Departure time :

Position visited

Name of pub

Drinks consumed

How many of you are there in total?

How many made it this far?

The next destination is

Place Name Here

Arrival time :

Departure time :

Position visited

Name of pub

Drinks consumed

How many of you are there in total?

How many made it this far?

The next destination is

At the same time you could complete these **Things To Do**
23: Get Arrested • 65: Shout 'Drinks Are on Me!' in a Pub or a Bar • 78: Drink a Vintage Wine • 81: Get Barred From a Pub or Bar

ENGLISH HERITAGE
JERRY SPRINGER
Talk show host ruined lives here
2004

Get Something Named After You

This is one way to make sure that you will be remembered long after you're dead and buried, but make sure you're around to witness the event and tick off the **Thing To Do** while you're still here.

John F. Kennedy had an airport named after him, **Princess Diana** has a rose named after her and even **Jesus Christ** has a country named after him (El Salvador, The Saviour). It seems you have to be someone pretty special (and usually dead) to have something named after you but if you've done half of the things in this book you've got a good chance of someone remembering you for one of them.

Get Named After ...

- A star – you can have a star named after you but do you really think the scientific community will refer to star UF-7320 as 'Dave'?
- A song – inspire someone enough for them to write a song about you. Make sure it paints you in a good light
- A child – if you're famous you can get thousands of children named after you; how many Kylies do you know?
- A stadium – pledge a shed-load of money to your favourite team and get their newly built stadium named after you

Things Not to be Named After
Hooligan: It is believed that the word hooligan derived from a rowdy Irish family that lived in London in the 1890s of the same name.

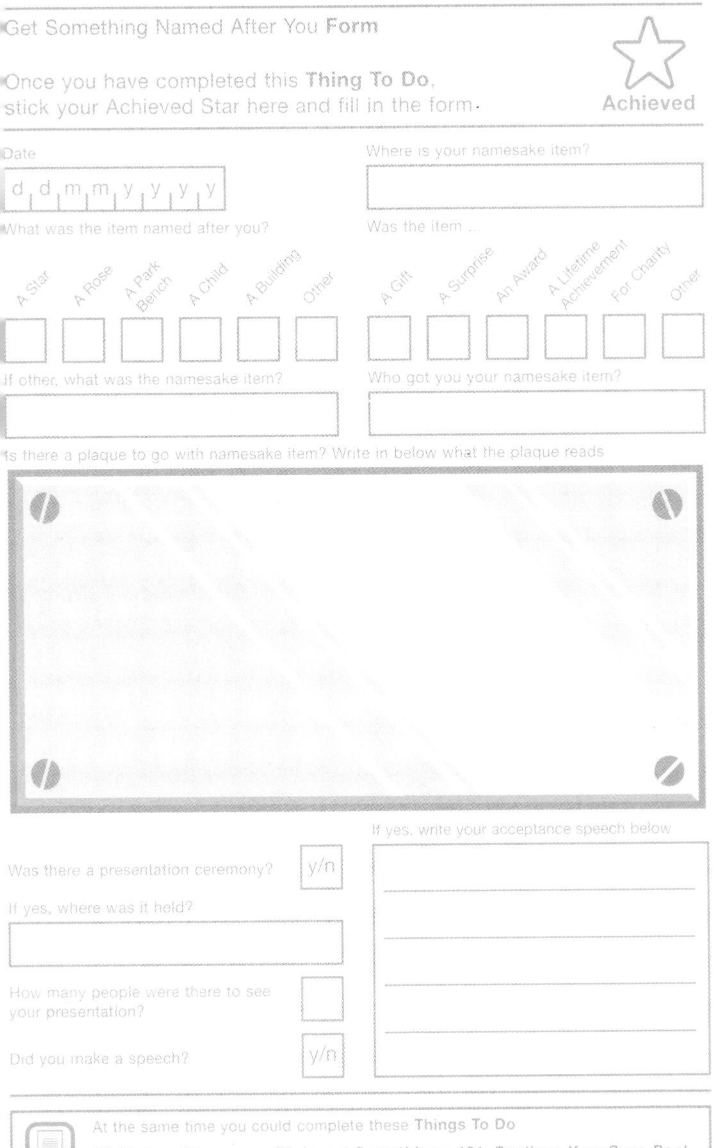
Get Something Named After You **Form**

Once you have completed this **Thing To Do**, stick your Achieved Star here and fill in the form.

Achieved

Date

d d m m y y y y

Where is your namesake item?

What was the item named after you?

A Star | A Rose | A Park Bench | A Child | A Building | Other

Was the item ...

A Gift | A Surprise | An Award | A Lifetime Achievement | For Charity | Other

If other, what was the namesake item?

Who got you your namesake item?

Is there a plaque to go with namesake item? Write in below what the plaque reads

Was there a presentation ceremony? y/n

If yes, where was it held?

How many people were there to see your presentation?

Did you make a speech? y/n

If yes, write your acceptance speech below

At the same time you could complete these **Things To Do**

05: Make a Discovery • 76: Invent Something • 101: Continue Your Gene Pool

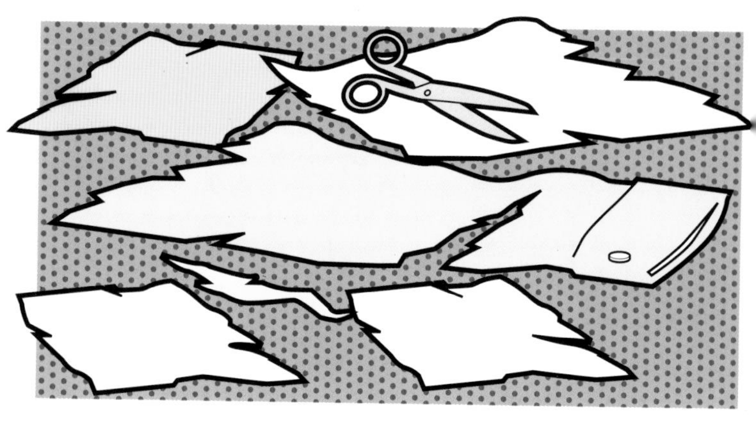

Get Revenge

Someone has done you wrong. You've lent a good friend money and you've never seen them again. You've had a job where they take everything and give nothing. You've been dumped by your partner and it turns out they were seeing your sister all along. You've been taken for a ride, anger has turned into hate, hate has turned into brooding and plotting. It's time to put the wrongs right.

Get Your Own Back

- Revenge against work – set up a website which has a similar address to the company you're seeking revenge from. Find a way for your site to be at the top of a search engine when the company is searched for. In your website tell everybody exactly how it is, have a facility so that other people who have been wronged can advertise their stories
- If dumped – arrange to take your ex out for dinner; towards the end of the meal head to the toilets; on the way past the bar order the most expensive bottle of champagne and have it delivered to the table. Bypass the toilet completely and walk straight out the front door, leaving your ex with the bill (see **Thing To Do** No. 45)
- Revenge of the Nerds – if you were bullied as a child for being a geek, find your tormentor and rub your current success and glamour in their face

---

Other Targets for Revenge Estate agents • Neighbours • The police • Traffic wardens • Your boss • Work colleagues • Teachers • Friends • Parents • The tax man • Road ragers • Mothers-in-law

Get Revenge **Form**

Once you have completed this **Thing To Do**,
stick your Achieved Star here and fill in the form

Achieved

How You Were Wronged

Date of incident

d d m m y y y y

Who wronged you?

What happened?

Your Revenge

Date of your revenge

d d m m y y y y

Who was your victim?

How did you get your revenge?

Did your revenge go as planned? y/n

If no, why not?

Did they get their own back on you? y/n

If yes, how did they do it?

At the same time you could complete these **Things To Do**
61: Get Away with the Perfect Practical Joke or Hoax • 72: Have Enough Money to Do All the Things on This List • 99: Confess

Be an Extra in a Film

Once you've made it onto your favourite TV show (see **Thing To Do** No. 35), take your new-found acting skills and move into the world of movies.

Go That Little Bit Extra

- Work your way into a talking part. You'll get more money and your name will climb higher up the credits at the end of the film
- Be in an epic battle scene. Don't get lost in the crowd, be noticeable. Either work your way to the front of the crowd, wear something really bright or die unconvincingly right in front of the camera
- Steal the scene. Bang your head like the stormtrooper in *Star Wars* or be the person wearing jeans in *Gladiator*. You'll never be forgotten, film geeks the world over will see to that

Build Your Part
During the filming of *The Alamo* John Wayne was accidentally stabbed in the chest by an over enthusiastic extra with a spear.

Be an Extra in a Film **Form**

Once you have completed this **Thing To Do**, stick your Achieved Star here and fill in the form

Achieved

Date and time you saw your appearance in a film

d d m m y y y y | :

What is the title of the film you were in?

Where did you see the film?

How long did filming take?

Days | Weeks | Hours

What was your total screen time?

Hours | Minutes | Seconds

How did you get picked to be in the film?

If your character had a name, what was it?

Did you have a speaking part? y/n

If yes, write some of your lines

Which famous people did you meet on set?

Place a screen grab of your appearance in the movie below

Was the film shot in your town? y/n

Did your name appear on the credits? y/n

At the same time you could complete these **Things To Do**

20: Get Backstage and Get Off with a Rock God • 29: Meet Your Idol • 35: Play a Part in Your Favourite TV Show • 44: Attend a Film Premiere

Live Out of a Van

Had enough of working every hour God sends? Fed up with being told what to do? It's time you had a break; take six weeks off, or six months if you have an understanding boss. Leave your cares behind and hit the open road, hire a camper van and travel the world. Leave all your home comforts behind you, trade your warm cosy bedroom for a freezing cold tin can.

On the Road

- If you're travelling around Australia buy a camper van instead of hiring; once you've finished your trip resell your van for the same amount you bought it for to other travellers. Look for adverts on hostel notice boards
- Beware, all camper vans are different. Check it has everything you need before buying
- Buy a Haynes manual. Camper vans are notoriously unreliable, so at least you'll have some backup if it does go wrong
- Add your own touches to the van (see **Thing To Do** No. 10) when you pass the vehicle on to the next owners they can add their mark and the next owners can add theirs, and so on. Part of you will be travelling Australia for years to come

Trailer Trash
Living in a van on a trailer park doesn't count. To qualify for this Thing To Do your van must have the ability to move.

Live Out of a Van **Form**

Once you have completed this **Thing To Do**, stick your Achieved Star here and fill in the form

Achieved

Date you set off

d d m m y y y y

Where did you set off from?

... And where did you end up?

Write in the names of the places you visited along the way ...

What were the coldest and hottest temperatures you experienced in the van?

°C

°C

Did you break down?

y/n

How many times?

times

How many miles did you cover?

Date you got back

d d m m y y y y

At the same time you could complete these **Things To Do**

36: Visit Every Country • 67: Visit ... • 71: Have Adventurous Sex • 58: Live in the Place You Love • 59: Leave a Job you Hate

Go on a Demonstration

If there is a cause you believe in, join the protest and swell the numbers. You've got a right to demonstrate so use it. Don't give in to apathy, make a stand!

Ways to Protest

- Tie yourself to a tree
- Live in a hole in the ground
- Stand in front of tanks
- Put flowers in guns
- Burn effigies of your leader
- Ransack fast-food chains

Fight the Power

- Design your own politically scathing T-shirt
- Invent new slogans such as 'A Bomb in the hand is worth two in the Bush'
- Invent new acronyms such as **WMD** (**W**eapons of **M**ass **D**estruction). Why isn't there one for **T**he **W**ar **A**gainst **T**error?

The Taste of Success

'We have heard you'

Roberto Goizueta, the chairman of the Coca-Cola Company in July 1985, speaking at a press conference on the massive opposition to the introduction of New Coke

When the Coca-Cola Company changed the taste of Coke due to the rise in popularity of their Pepsi rivals in 1985, the population of America wouldn't have it

Demonstrations were held, anti-New Coke groups were formed, and protests were held at the head-quarters of Coca-Cola

Within two weeks of its introduction, after spending millions on developing the new taste of Coke, the original taste of Coca-Cola was reintroduced

Twenty years later Coca-Cola is still at the top of the soft drink pile, funny that

Worlds Biggest Demonstration

The Anti-war against Iraq demonstrations held mid February 2003. Millions of people took part in the biggest worldwide demonstration ever seen.

Go on a Demonstration **Form**

Once you have completed this **Thing To Do**, stick your Achieved Star here and fill in the form

Achieved

Date of demonstration

d d m m y y y y :

What was the demonstration for?

Did you have a placard?

y/n If yes, what did it say? Write your slogans on the placards

Was there a march?

y/n From ...

To ...

How many people took part?

Did you see yourself on the news? y/n

Was it peaceful? y/n

If no, were you involved in the trouble? y/n

Did the demonstration do any good? y/n

If you had a badge what did it say?

Did you have a message on your T-shirt? y/n

If yes, what did it say?

Were you involved in the following:

Burning flags	Graffiti	Love-in
Tree protests	Rioting	Free-Love
Underground protests	Looting	Burning bras

At the same time you could complete these **Things To Do**

10: Leave Your Mark in Graffiti • 23: Get Arrested • 91: Publish a Cult Website • 63: Make the Front Page of a National Newspaper • 95: Get Revenge

Confess

Secrets. Everyone has them. We carry the burden of our secrets around with us every day – they're always with us. If you're lucky enough to forget about them you know it's only a matter of time before it all comes flooding back and the guilt is even stronger than before.

Things can go too far and, once they have, you have a simple choice, confess or lie. Nine out of ten times, we lie. Our tiny lie will solve the problem in the short term but then our little lie gathers momentum and before you know it, it's too late, it's turned into a monster and you're swept up in a huge web of lies. It's time to confess. Use the form opposite to confess your sins.

Get It Off Your Chest

- Visit the confessional box at church. Confess your sins to the priest and make some even worse sins up. The priest is obliged to keep the secrets to himself (and God). Leave the confessional box a new person, and leave the priest with an agonising choice. Should he keep it to himself or should he tell the police about the murder, scandal and misery that you've just owned up to?

Salem Witch Trials In 1692, a group of girls suddenly suffered from convulsions, hallucinations and talking oddly. Witchcraft was blamed and trials were held. 19 people were executed for not confessing to being a witch, those that confessed went to jail. It has recently been concluded that the girls were poisoned by eating contaminated rye bread containing ergot, a fungus that lives in rye. The hallucinogen LSD is found in ergot.

Confess **Form**

Once you have completed this **Thing To Do**,
stick your Achieved Star here and fill in the form

Achieved

I Confess ...

your signature

witness signature

At the same time you could complete these **Things To Do**
07: Be Part of a Threesome • 61: Get Away with the Perfect Practical Joke or Hoax • 95: Get Revenge

ER
Happy 100th Birthday
from Queen Liz

Reach 100 Years of Age

The world is a dangerous place; everything is out to get you. One wrong step into the street, and it's the end of the road. Have an accident cleaning the windows and it's curtains.

There are spiders and snakes out there with enough venom to kill you ten times over, the cold, the heat, hereditary diseases, your pets, your staircase and pretty much everything in your own home. Even something as innocent as a sandwich has got numerous ways to kill; bite too much off and you could choke; the contents could poison you; and the van they're in might kill you on their way to the shop.

Death is a constant shadow for us all but you've got to keep one step ahead if you want to reach one hundred years of age; keep on the right side of death and don't deviate. Where's the fun in that? Well, OK, defy death once in a while.

Who Wants To Live For Ever?

- Embrace old age when it comes. Ignore people and claim you're deaf; get your own way – who's going to argue with a pensioner? And if you're in pain shout, 'God! I'll be with you soon!'

One Hundred Years Is Equivalent to:
10 decades, 1,200 months, 5,217.75 weeks, 36,524.22 days, 876,581.28 hours, 52,594,876.6 minutes and 3.1556926×10^9 seconds (approximately 3.1 billion seconds)

Reach 100 Years of Age **Form**

Once you have completed this **Thing To Do**, stick your Achieved Star here and fill in the form

Achieved

A TIMELINE OF YOUR ACHIEVEMENTS

Enlarge the form and put it on your wall to chart your achievements. Write against the corresponding age when you completed the Things To Do; also add your other achievements and life-changing events. Fill in the star on your 100th birthday

0 1 2 3 4 5 6 7 8 9 10 11 12 13 14 15 16 17 18 19 20 21 22 23 24 25

26 27 28 29 30 31 32 33 34 35 36 37 38 39 40 41 42 43 44 45 46 47 48 49 50

51 52 53 54 55 56 57 58 59 60 61 62 63 64 65 66 67 68 69 70 71 72 73 74 75

76 77 78 79 80 81 82 83 84 85 86 87 88 89 90 91 92 93 94 95 96 97 98 99 100

What is your greatest achievement?

What would you have liked to have done but didn't?

At the same time you could complete these **Things To Do**

52: Read the Greatest Books Ever Written • 58: Live in the Place You Love

Continue Your Gene Pool

We were all born with a purpose, and that purpose is to procreate. It's in our nature.

On 12 October 1999, the six billionth person was born. People are living longer than they ever have done and the population is constantly on the increase. In twenty-four hours, approximately 237,000 people are born and 140,000 die. We're filling the world up with our children, but at least there are plenty of grandparents to babysit when you go out for the night. But don't let these facts and figures put you off; see it as 6 billion playmates your child hasn't met yet.

As for the population growth in the future, the seven billionth person is expected in 2012.

Things To Do

- Pass this book on to your children so they have a record of all the things you got up to when you were cool

Look Back to the Past
Discover your origins. Research your family tree and discover long-lost relatives, see if you're in line for a huge family inheritance or if you are in line for the throne.

Continue Your Gene Pool **Form**

Once you have completed this **Thing To Do**, stick your Achieved Star here and fill in the form

Achieved

Name of First Child

Date of Birth

d d m m y y y y

Time of Birth

Sex m/f

Weight kg

Size cm

First Word:

What do you think they'll be when they grow up?

Place a photo here

Name of Second Child

Date of Birth

d d m m y y y y

Time of Birth

Sex m/f

Weight kg

Size cm

First Word:

What do you think they'll be when they grow up?

Place a photo here

At the same time you could complete these **Things To Do**
18: Study the *Kama Sutra* and Put Theory into Practice • 62: Join the Mile High Club • 71: Have Adventurous Sex

Appendix

Over the following pages are items to help you get more out of your **101 Things To Do Before You Die** manual

Your **Things To Do**

- List the things that you'd like to do that weren't mentioned in the book

Write Your Own **Thing To Do**

- The **Things To Do** in this book are a guideline to the things you could achieve before it's too late. If you disagree with some of the suggestions listed in this book, the next two pages are designed for you to write your own **Thing To Do**. Once you have achieved your **Thing To Do** write your results in the space provided. Devise your own form listing times, dates and other details of interest
- Place your new **Thing To Do** over an existing one that you know you will never complete

Pocket-sized Check List

- A handy check list to keep with you twenty-four seven. Compare with your friends or use it to show that you're an active person who's not at all square

Extra Paper

- Photocopy the extra pages so that when you run out of space on a particular form, you can use the extra pages to continue writing. Attach the extra pages to the relevant form

Acknowledgements

- A chance for you to thank all those people who have helped you achieve the goals mentioned in this book

About the Author

- Fill in your own details

Your Things To Do

Add the **Things To Do** that you want to do before you die that weren't mentioned in the book

Thing To Do 1

Thing To Do 2

Thing To Do 3

Thing To Do 4

Thing To Do 5

Thing To Do 6

Thing To Do 7

Thing To Do 8

Thing To Do 9

Thing To Do 10

Enter your favourite **Thing To Do** that wasn't mentioned in the book into the next double spread

Title for Your **Thing To Do**

Choose a **Thing To Do** that you'd like to complete but that wasn't featured in the book and write your own information about your **Thing To Do** over this text.

Draw, in the space provided above, an illustration relating to your **Thing To Do**. Place the title for your **Thing To Do** in the yellow bar at the top and decide which category your **Thing** should fit into from Achievement, Entertainment, Excitement, Life Management, Miscellaneous, Nature, Recklessness, Relationships, Sport and Travel.

On the right hand side, describe what happened when you completed your **Thing To Do**.

Other Possible **Things To Do**

- Climb Everest
- Steal Your Own Christmas Tree
- Make a Number One Record
- Get Bitten by a Shark and Survive
- Eat Something That's Still Alive
- Rule the World

Interesting Fact
Write an interesting fact about your **Thing To Do** in this space provided.

Form

Once you have written your **Thing To Do**, stick your Achieved Star here and design your own form

Achieved

At the same time you could complete these **Things To Do**

How to Use Your Pocket-sized Check List

Follow the following instructions and you can keep track of your completed **Things To Do** at a moment's notice.

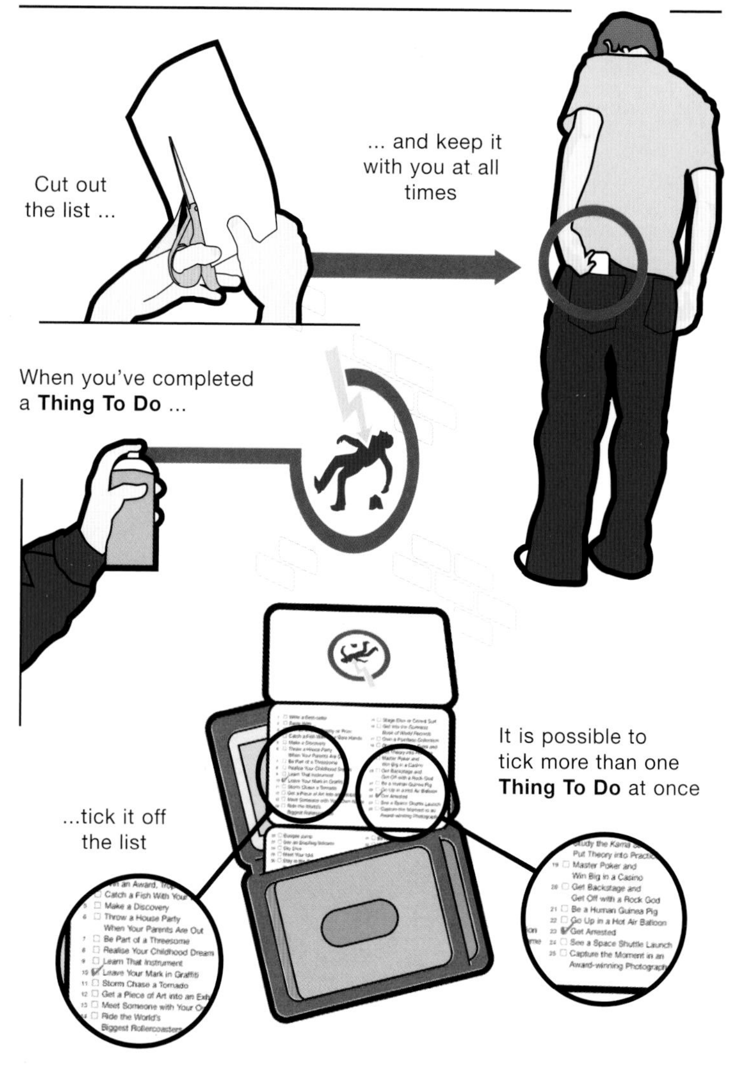

Cut out the list ...
... and keep it with you at all times
When you've completed a **Thing To Do** ...
...tick it off the list
It is possible to tick more than one **Thing To Do** at once

Small print: Keep this list with you at all times. Use every opportunity to complete the **Things To Do** on this list. This card cannot be used as credit for goods; if you attempt to do so you will almost certainly complete **Thing To Do** No. 23.

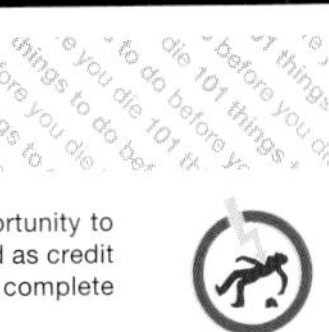

24-hour helpline call 0800 000 101

1 ☐ Write a Best-seller
2 ☐ Swim With ...
3 ☐ Win an Award, Trophy or Prize
4 ☐ Catch a Fish With Your Bare Hands
5 ☐ Make a Discovery
6 ☐ Throw a House Party When Your Parents Are Out
7 ☐ Be Part of a Threesome
8 ☐ Realise Your Childhood Dream
9 ☐ Learn That Instrument
10 ☐ Leave Your Mark in Graffiti
11 ☐ Storm Chase a Tornado
12 ☐ Get a Piece of Art into an Exhibition
13 ☐ Meet Someone with Your Own Name
14 ☐ Ride the World's Biggest Rollercoasters
15 ☐ Stage Dive or Crowd Surf
16 ☐ Get into the Guinness *Book of World Records*
17 ☐ Own a Pointless Collection
18 ☐ Study the *Kama Sutra* and Put Theory into Practice
19 ☐ Master Poker and Win Big in a Casino
20 ☐ Get Backstage and Get Off with a Rock God
21 ☐ Be a Human Guinea Pig
22 ☐ Go Up in a Hot Air Balloon
23 ☐ Get Arrested
24 ☐ See a Space Shuttle Launch
25 ☐ Capture the Moment in an Award-winning Photograph

Check List

26 ☐ Bungee Jump
27 ☐ See an Erupting Volcano
28 ☐ Sky Dive
29 ☐ Meet Your Idol
30 ☐ Stay in the Best Suite in a Five Star Hotel
31 ☐ Experience Weightlessness
32 ☐ See the Aurora Borealis
33 ☐ Get to Score a Hole in One
34 ☐ Design Your Own Cocktail
35 ☐ Play a Part in Your Favourite TV Show
36 ☐ Visit Every Country
37 ☐ Make Fire Without Matches
38 ☐ See These Animals in the Wild ...
39 ☐ Go to the Dogs
40 ☐ Get a Free Upgrade on a Plane
41 ☐ Be Friends With Your Ex
42 ☐ Hit Your Targets
43 ☐ Throw a Dart into a Map and Travel to Where it Lands
44 ☐ Attend a Film Premiere
45 ☐ Do a Runner From a Fancy Restaurant
46 ☐ Scuba Dive
47 ☐ Milk a Cow
48 ☐ Be Present When Your Country Wins the World Cup
49 ☐ See Both Solar and Lunar Eclipses
50 ☐ Write Your Name Over a Star on the Walk of Fame
51 ☐ Learn Another Language
52 ☐ Read the Greatest Books Ever Written

53 ☐ Complete a Coast to Coast Road Trip Across America
54 ☐ Make at Least One Huge Purchase You Can't Afford
55 ☐ Score the Winning Goal/Try/Basket
56 ☐ Gatecrash a Fancy Party
57 ☐ See the All-time Greatest Films
58 ☐ Live in the Place You Love
59 ☐ Leave a Job You Hate
60 ☐ Take Part in an Police Line-up
61 ☐ Get Away with the Perfect Practical Joke or Hoax
62 ☐ Join the Mile High Club
63 ☐ Make the Front Page of a National Newspaper
64 ☐ Drive a Car at Top Speed
65 ☐ Shout 'Drinks Are on Me!' in a Pub or a Bar
66 ☐ Be Part of a Flash Mob
67 ☐ Visit ...
68 ☐ Save Someone's Life
69 ☐ In Various Languages, Learn to ...
70 ☐ Invent a Word That Makes it into the Dictionary
71 ☐ Have Adventurous Sex
72 ☐ Have Enough Money to Do All the Things on This List
73 ☐ Stand on the International Date Line
74 ☐ Learn to Fly a Plane
75 ☐ Get a Tattoo and/or a Piercing
76 ☐ Invent Something

77 ☐ Learn Astronomy and Read the Night Sky
78 ☐ Drink a Vintage Wine
79 ☐ Answer a Personal Ad
80 ☐ Spend Christmas on the Beach
81 ☐ Get Barred From a Pub or Bar
82 ☐ Build Your Own House
83 ☐ Skinny Dip at Midnight
84 ☐ Sell All Your Junk on eBay and Make a Profit
85 ☐ Visit the World's Tallest Buildings
86 ☐ Run a Marathon
87 ☐ Conquer Your Fear
88 ☐ Get Married Unusually
89 ☐ Throw Away the Instant Noodles
90 ☐ Join the 16-Mile High Club
91 ☐ Publish a Cult Website
92 ☐ Own an Original Work of Art
93 ☐ Complete the Monopoly Board Pub Crawl
94 ☐ Get Something Named After You
95 ☐ Get Revenge
96 ☐ Be an Extra in a Film
97 ☐ Live Out of a Van
98 ☐ Go on a Demonstration
99 ☐ Confess
100 ☐ Reach 100 Years of Age
101 ☐ Continue Your Gene Pool

Write the name of the Thing To Do title here

Cut Here

Cut Here

Extra Paper

Write the name of the Thing To Do title here

Cut Here

Cut Here

Thank Yous and Noteworthy Acknowledgements

Write your own acknowledgements
over the example below

Thank You to: my parents for carrying on their gene pool so successfully. Jane Horne and Ricky Harrison for their help, patience and their house

A Huge Thanks to the Following at Bloomsbury Publishing: Mary Davis, Rosemary Davidson, James Spackman, Mike Jones, Ele Fountain, Helen Szirtes, Holly Roberts, Will Webb, Nathan Buron, Yeti McCaldin, Isabella Pereira, Hugo de Klee, Nicky Thompson and Polly Napper

Family and Friends, Thanks to: Rob Ellis & Karly Hammond, Simon & Charlotte Warren, Jan Williamson & Carl Smyth, Stephen & Amanda Laverick, Sam, Ben, Sue & Mick Allen, Jess McClelland, Jim Newbery, Edward Faulkner & Clare Taylor, Allison Chamberlain, Katy Thompson, Zoe Balmforth, Hazel Chiu & Audley Jarvis, Pat Virdee, Rob Hackett, Paul Johnson, Sue, Alyn & Alex Ostle and a mystery wedding guy whose name escapes me

Thanks to: the Mess Cafe in Hackney, the Nellie Dean in Soho and the Roebuck in Reading

A Special Thanks to: Eleanor Bursey & Sanchia Lovell for the free coffee

Thanks, But No Thanks to: Mark Rusher

About the Author

Write your details over the top of the example below

Place a passport photo of yourself here

Name

Richard Horne

Age

30

Date of birth

02061973

Occupation(s)

Designer

Illustrator

Place of birth

Guisborough

Place of upbringing

Middlesbrough

Place of residence

Hackney, London

Which country do you live in?

England

How many Things To Do have you completed before you start?

15

How many Things To Do have you partially completed?

11

How many Things To Do do you think you will complete?

97

Your story so far

Richard Horne is a designer of record covers (Tom Jones and Faith No More), book jackets (Paul Morley, Sean French and the Harry Potter series) and websites (Margaret Atwood – www.oryxandcrake.co.uk, Sophie Dahl – www.dancingeyes.net and Ethan Hawke – www.ashwednesday.co.uk), as well as a greetings card and magazine illustrator (Guardian and Sugar). A self-confessed chancer, this is his first bestseller.

What will your next book be?

My Second Best-seller

Achieved Stars